# *Schritte* 4
## international

### Glossary XXL
### Deutsch–Englisch
### German–English

## Hueber Verlag

**English Translation and Adaption:**
Jeannie Sanke

**Authors:**
Sophie Caesar (Familiarity and Understanding)
María Jesús Gil Valdés (Listening and Pronunciation)
Christiane Seuthe (Forms and Structures)
Wilfried Völker (Historical Fragments)

With articles from
Hans Christian Hagedorn (Chapter 8/Hauff)
Dolores Rodríguez Cemillán (Chapter 9/music)

**Quellenverzeichnis**
Fotos:
Umschlag/Seite 4/5: alle Fotos © Alexander Keller, München
Seite 14: © culture-images/Lebrecht Music & Arts
Seite 16 und 19: © picture-alliance/akg-images
Seite 28: oben © Siemens AG, München/Berlin, unten: © EFA - Museum für deutsche Automobilgeschichte
Seite 29: © fotolia/saschi79
Seite 30: oben © panthermedia/Karin L.; unten © Take2 Designagentur, www.take2-design.de
Seite 31: © picture-alliance/Jazz Archiv
Seite 32: oben © picture-alliance/dpa; unten und Seite 33: © Gutenberg-Museum Mainz. Museum für Buch-, Druck- und Schriftgeschichte
Seite 44: © BilderBox/Erwin Wodicka
Seite 45: oben © culture images/wa; Mitte © picture-alliance/dpa; unten © panthermedia/Marcus L.

Seite 46: © MEV
Seite 58: © picture-alliance/akg-images
Seite 60: © panthermedia/Rolf Georg B.
Seite 61: © iStockphoto/Damir Wallener
Seite 62: © picture-alliance/MAXPPP
Seite 71: © BallinStadt, Hamburg
Seite 72: © picture-alliance/Sven Simon
Seite 73/74: © MHV
Seite 75: © panthermedia/Bernd K.
Seite 82: links © Foto SBB; rechts © Deutsche Bahn AG/Günter Jazbec
Seite 83: oben © picture-alliance/dpa unten © University of Texas at Austin
Seite 85: © Bridgeman Art Library
Seite 96: © panthermedia/Michael N.
Seite 97: © Bayerische Schlösserverwaltung
Seite 99: © fotolia/Martina Berg

3. 2. 1.                    Die letzten Ziffern
2014 13 12 11 10           bezeichnen Zahl und Jahr des Druckes.
Alle Drucke dieser Auflage können, da unverändert,
nebeneinander benutzt werden.
1. Auflage
© 2010 Hueber Verlag, 85737 Ismaning, Deutschland
Zeichnungen: Jörg Saupe, Düsseldorf
Layout: Erwin Schmid, Hueber Verlag, Ismaning
Satz: Typosatz W. Namisla GmbH, München
Redaktion: CoLibris-Lektorat Dr. Barbara Welzel, Göttingen
Druck und Bindung: Ludwig Auer GmbH, Donauwörth
Printed in Germany
ISBN 978-3-19-451854-4

# Preface

**Dear Learner,**

in this **XXL Glossary** you will find, as its title suggests, much more than just a glossary. Each chapter includes the following sections:

## Vocabulary

All new words are presented in the order in which they appear in both the course book and the workbook, page-by-page, then alphabetically. Unlike a dictionary, this glossary allows you to learn words in context so that their meaning is far more real to you than a dictionary entry.

## Forms and Structures

In this section, we explain grammar based on concrete examples from the course book and compare and contrast the structures with those of English. As the course proceeds, you will find continued reference in newer sections to material in previous chapters to help reinforce your understanding and mastery of these points. We also make a point of pointing out differences between English and German that can potentially hinder your understanding or lead you into traps. We have also included additional **translation exercises** in each chapter to help you get a better sense of your progress and mastery, allowing you to see more how German and English are similar and different.

## Listening and Pronunciation

As important as grammar, structure and vocabulary are, without knowing the sound system, they are of no use. In this section, we aim to give you the tools you will need not only to recognize the sounds of German, but to reproduce them so that you can be understood, even when your structural knowledge is weak.

## Familiarity and Understanding

No language exists apart from the culture in which it is couched. Here you will learn about the German-speaking areas of the world, their literature and arts, and aspects of daily life. This section also aspires to help you avoid common missteps that many foreigners and learners make.

## Historical Fragments

As in previous volumes, each chapter provides an overview of a particular chapter of German history. Likewise, you will note as you progress through this volume, topics move in reverse through time. While this might seem counterproductive at first, it will allow you in many ways to take advantage of what you might already know to build a more complete understanding as you venture further into the unknown. Topics in this volume concentrate on the earliest recorded periods of German history, reaching back through the Holy Roman Empire to the Roman occupation of the German-speaking areas.

## Self-Evaluation

At the end of each chapter, you have the opportunity to evaluate your progress on the objectives in each unit, allowing you to give extra attention and/or seek extra help in areas where you are not as confident in your new skills.

We hope that you find this volume helps you learn German with greater ease and more enjoyment, and we wish you every success.

Sincerely,

the authors and editors

# Contents

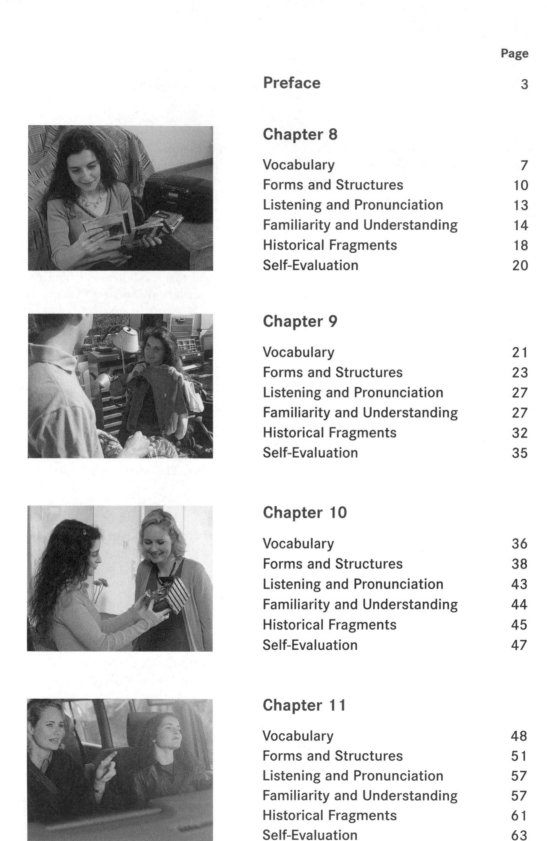

# Contents

Page

## Chapter 12

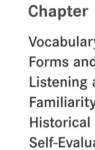
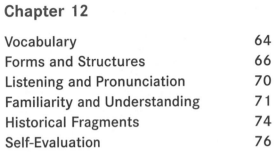

## Chapter 13

## Chapter 14

| Kursbuch | Textbook |
|---|---|
| **Die erste Stunde im Kurs** | **The first hour of class** |
| *aus aller Welt* | *from throughout the world* |
| gemeinsam | common, shared |
| *der Gesprächspartner, –* | *conversation partner* |
| *die Weile (Sg)* | *while* |

| **Seite 8** | **page 8** |
|---|---|
| sauer | here: angry, peeved |

| **Seite 9** | **page 9** |
|---|---|
| gegenüber | across the way |
| *der Klavierspieler, –* | *piano player* |
| *die Matheaufgabe, -n* | *math assignment* |
| *das Nachbarhaus, ¨er* | *neighbor's house* |
| *der Skateboardplatz, ¨e* | *skateboarding area* |
| das Stück, -e | piece, selection |

| **Seite 10** | **page 10** |
|---|---|
| *das Drehbuch, ¨er* | *script* |
| *enthalten* | *to contain* |
| Fall: auf keinen Fall | case, event: in no case, by no means |
| die Luft, ¨e | air |
| *die Regieanweisung, -en* | *stage direction* |
| *spätestens* | *at the latest* |
| *das Süße (Sg)* | *sweet thing, sweet stuff* |
| verliebt | in love |

| **Seite 11** | **page 11** |
|---|---|
| das Blatt, ¨er | here: sheet (of paper) |
| das Klavier, -e | piano |
| die Ruhe (Sg) | rest, quiet |
| die Streichholzschachtel, -n | matchbox |
| *die Wunschliste, -n* | *wish list* |

| **Seite 12** | **page 12** |
|---|---|
| einverstanden | agreed |
| *die LAN-Party, -s* | *LAN party* |
| mit·gehen, er ist mitgegangen | to go along |
| prima | excellent, great, awesome |
| *der Tango-Schuh, -e* | *tango shoe* |
| vor·schlagen, du schlägst vor, er schlägt vor, er hat vorgeschlagen | to suggest |

| **Seite 13** | **page 13** |
|---|---|
| die Ausstellung, -en | exhibition |
| der Autor, -en | author |
| *der Dienstbereich, -e* | *area of service* |
| *die DVD, -s* | *DVD* |
| *die Eisdisco, -s* | *disco on ice* |
| *das Eisstadion, Eisstadien* | *ice arena* |
| *die Eröffnung, -en* | *opening (of an event)* |
| die Erzählung, -en | story, narrative |
| die Feuerwehr (Sg) | fire department |
| der Freitagabend, -e | Friday evening |
| das Gesicht, -er | face |
| *das Heimatmuseum, -museen* | *museum of local history* |
| *der Hobbyfotograf, -en* | *amateur photographer* |
| klassisch | classical |
| die Kneipe, -n | bar, pub |
| die Leitung, -en | direction |
| *die Lesung, -en* | *reading* |
| das Lokal, -e | pub, saloon |
| die Lüge, -n | lie |
| die Macht, ¨e | power |
| *die Nachbarschaft (Sg)* | *neighborhood* |
| *das Nachtgespräch, -e* | *nighttime conversation* |
| *das Orchester, –* | *orchestra* |
| *die Promenade, -n* | *promenade, avenue* |
| *die Reederei, -en* | *steamship line* |
| die Reihe, -n | here: series |
| *die Rundfahrt, -en* | *tour* |
| der Senior, -en | senior (citizen) |
| die Studentenermäßigung, -en | student discount |
| *der Tag der offenen Tür* | *open house* |
| die Veranstaltung, -en | event |
| *der Veranstaltungskalender, –* | *calendar of events* |
| verbringen, er hat verbracht | to spend (time) |
| *der Verkauf, ¨e* | *sale* |
| *das Weihnachtsstück, -e* | *Christmas piece (of music)* |
| das Werk, -e | work (of art, music, etc.) |
| *die Wochenendaktivität, -en* | *weekend activity* |

| **Seite 14** | **page 14** |
|---|---|
| außerhalb | outside of, beyond |
| *ein·schreiben (sich), er hat sich eingeschrieben* | *to register* |
| *der Filmemacher, –* | *filmmaker* |
| *die Filmreihe, -n* | *film series* |
| *die Filmwerkstatt, ¨en* | *film workshop/factory* |
| historisch | historic, historical |
| lebenslang | lifelong |
| die Mittagszeit, -en | noontime, lunchtime |
| *das Open Air, -s* | *open air* |
| *der Radiosender, –* | *radio station* |
| der Rundfunk (Sg) | radio (technology/broadcast system) |

| | |
|---|---|
| das Sommersemester, – | summer semester |
| die Tombola, -s | raffle |
| das Tor, -e | gate |
| die Totalrenovierung, -en | complete (gut) renovation |
| der Veranstaltungstipp, -s | event tip |
| vielseitig | multifaceted |
| die Volkshochschule, -n | school offering adult/continuing education classes |
| die Wiedereröffnung, -en | reopening |
| der Ziegenstall, ⸚e | goat barn |
| zuvor | before (this time) |

## Seite 15 — page 15

| | |
|---|---|
| an·nehmen, du nimmst an, er nimmt an, er hat angenommen | here: to accept |
| äußern | to express |

## Seite 16 — page 16

| | |
|---|---|
| altmodisch | old-fashioned |
| die Bibel, -n | Bible |
| die Definition, -en | definition |
| das Glossar, -e | glossary |
| körperlich | physical |
| das Märchen, – | fairy tale |
| nach·lesen, du liest nach, er liest nach, er hat nachgelesen | to read up on something |
| optimistisch | optimistic |
| der Tag des Herrn | the Lord's day |
| der Vegetarier, – | vegetarian |
| verwenden | to use |
| der Sonntagsbraten, – | Sunday roast |
| der Sonntagsfahrer, – | Sunday driver; inexperienced driver |
| das Sonntagskind, -er | Sunday's child |
| das Sonntags-Wort, -e | Sunday word |

## Seite 17 — page 17

| | |
|---|---|
| aus·denken (sich), er hat sich ausgedacht | to think up, come up with |
| die Ausgabe, -n | edition |
| der Autofahrer, – | auto driver |
| der Kirchgang (Sg) | going to church |
| mehrmals | often, repeatedly |
| der Sonntagsanzug, ⸚e | Sunday suit (Sunday best) |
| die Sonntagsbeilage, -n | Sunday extra section in the Saturday paper |
| die Sonntagsblume, -n | Sunday flower |
| der Sonntagsjäger, – | Sunday hunter (inexperienced) |
| das Sonntagskleid, -er | Sunday dress (Sunday best) |

| | |
|---|---|
| die Sonntagslangeweile (Sg) | Sunday boredom |
| der Sonntagsmaler, – | Sunday painter (inexperienced) |
| die Sonntagsrede, -n | Sunday sermon |
| der Sonntagsredner, – | one who does not practice what s/he preaches |
| der Sonntagsspaziergang, ⸚e | Sunday constitutional, Sunday walk |
| die Sonntagszeitung, -en | Sunday paper |
| ungeübt | not practiced, unskilled |
| unsicher | uncertain |

## Arbeitsbuch — Workbook

### Seite 82 — page 82

| | |
|---|---|
| der Abteilungsleiter, – | department head |
| der Postangestellte, -n | postal clerk |

### Seite 83 — page 83

| | |
|---|---|
| eiskalt | ice cold |
| herum·laufen, du läufst herum, er läuft herum, er ist herumgelaufen | to run around |
| das Musikstück, -e | piece of music |
| der Videofilm, -e | video film |

### Seite 84 — page 84

| | |
|---|---|
| Brasilien (Sg) | Brazil |

### Seite 85 — page 85

| | |
|---|---|
| betont | emphasized |
| der Krimi, -s | detective or murder mystery |

### Seite 86 — page 86

| | |
|---|---|
| der Sonntagmorgen, – | Sunday morning |
| das Stadion, Stadien | stadium |

### Seite 87 — page 87

| | |
|---|---|
| der Donnerstagabend, -e | Thursday evening |

### Seite 88 — page 88

| | |
|---|---|
| das Aufgabenblatt, ⸚er | exercise sheet |
| die Fahrradtour, -en | bicycle tour, trip |
| die Schifffahrt (Sg) | boat trip |

| Seite 89 | page 89 |
|---|---|
| *der Bau, -ten* | *here: building* |
| die Diskothek, -en | discotheque |
| *die Entwicklung, -en* | *development* |
| die Familienfeier, -n | family celebration, party |
| *der Freizeitpark, -s* | *park with freetime activities* |
| *die Galerie, -n* | *gallery* |
| *geschichtlich* | *historical* |
| *die Internet-Homepage, -s* | *internet homepage* |
| kulturell | cultural |
| *das Kloster, ⸚* | *cloister, monastery* |
| *der Link, -s* | *link* |
| *die Städtetour, -en* | *city tour* |
| *der Stadtrundgang, ⸚e* | *city tour (walking)* |
| *der Themenrundgang, ⸚e* | *themed tour* |
| *der Tiergarten, ⸚* | *zoo, animal park* |
| *touristisch* | *tourist (adj.)* |
| *die Zimmervermittlung, -en* | *agency for booking rooms* |

## 1 The conjunction *trotzdem (Konjunktion „trotzdem")*

examples

*Das Wetter ist nicht besonders schön.*
***Trotzdem** wollen Kurt und Susanne wegfahren.*

The weather is not particularly nice. In spite of that, Kurt and Susanne want to go somewhere.

*Sabine macht nie die Hausaufgaben.*
***Trotzdem** besteht sie alle Prüfungen.*

Sabine never does her homework. Despite of that, she passes all her exams.

*Trotzdem* connects two principle statements to express an unexpected outcome.
Though *trotzdem* is presented here as a conjunction, it does not function in the same manner as coordinating or subordinating conjunctions, but more like an adverb. Notice that when *trotzdem* is used, the verb is still in second position, but the subject is after the verb, not before it.

Remember that *und* and *denn* coordinate two main clauses, and word order does not change:
*Sabine besteht alle Prüfungen, denn sie lernt viel.*
The conunctions *weil* and *wenn* connect main and subordinate clauses, and the conjugated verb in the subordinate clause is in the final position:
*Sabine besteht alle Prüfungen, weil sie viel lernt.*

In contrast, when using *trotzdem*, it becomes a part of the second clause, the one expressing the unexpected consequence. Like an adverb, then, it takes position either at the beginning of the clause (followed by the verb and then the subject) or it follows the verb:

*Sabine macht nie die Hausaufgaben.*

***Trotzdem** besteht sie alle Prüfungen.*
*Sie besteht **trotzdem** alle Prüfungen.*

## 2 *Konjunktiv II:* wish *(Konjunktiv II: Wunsch)*

examples

*Wir fahren nie ohne die Kinder weg.*
*Wir **würden** gern mal wieder allein **wegfahren**.*

We never go away without the children. We would like to go away alone again.

*Mama will, dass ich ihr helfe. Dabei **wäre** ich jetzt so gern auf dem Skateboardplatz!*

Mama wants me to help her. I would so love to be at the skateboard park!

*Ich habe kaum Zeit für mich.*
*Ich **hätte** gern mal ein bisschen Ruhe.*

I hardly have time for myself. I'd love to have a little peace and quiet.

As we do in English with the subjunctive, German uses the *Konjunktiv II* to express hypothetical or contrary-to-fact statements. When expressing a wish or desire for something, again, German uses the *Konjunktiv II* as English would the subjunctive. Very often, the subjunctive verb form in a wish statement is accompanied by *gern*.

In *Schritte international 1*, Chapter 6, we already encountered *möchten* (the *Konjunktiv II* of the verb *mögen*) for use in formulating a wish or for making a polite request:
*Ich möchte gern eine Cola.*

The same idea can also be expressed this way:
*Ich hätte gern eine Cola.*

In *Schritte international 2*, Chapter 12, we also saw the *Konjunktiv II* used for expressing other polite requests:
*Würden Sie bitte einen Moment warten?*
*Könntest du mal den Reparaturservice anrufen?*

In the majority of cases where a request or desire is expressed, the *Konjunktiv II* is formed using *würde* – as an auxiliary with the infinitive of the verb in question:

*warten → ich würde warten*
*wegfahren → ich würde wegfahren*

In contrast, however, the verbs *haben*, *sein* and the modal verbs use their individual *Konjunktiv II* forms:

*haben → ich hätte*
*sein → ich wäre*

As you can see in the following table, these forms bear a striking resemblance to those of the *Präteritum*. In the case of *haben*, the only difference is the *Umlaut* which changes the vowel. In the *Konjunktiv II* forms of *sein*, not only is there an *Umlaut*, but the endings have an *-e-* before the *Präteritum* ending, whether a zero ending or a consonant. This *-e-* is often omitted in second-person forms (*du*, *ihr*) in speaking.

|  | *Präteritum* | *Konjunktiv* | *Präteritum* | *Konjunktiv* |
|---|---|---|---|---|
| *ich* | *war* | *wäre* | *hatte* | *hätte* |
| *du* | *warst* | *wär(e)st* | *hattest* | *hättest* |
| *er/sie/es* | *war* | *wäre* | *hatte* | *hätte* |
| *wir* | *waren* | *wären* | *hatten* | *hätten* |
| *ihr* | *wart* | *wär(e)t* | *hattet* | *hättet* |
| *sie/Sie* | *waren* | *wären* | *hatten* | *hätten* |

## 3   *Konjunktiv II:* suggestion *(Konjunktiv II: Vorschlag)*

examples   *Wir könnten mal wieder zusammen was unternehmen.*    We could do something together again sometime.

*Du könntest doch Mathe lernen.*    You could study your math.

The *Konjunktiv* can also express suggestions, as the subjunctive does in English. In both languages, the *Konjunktiv* of the verb *können* (can) is used. The *Konjunktiv II* forms of *können* are also built upon the *Präteritum* forms, then adding an *Umlaut*:

|  | *Präteritum* | *Konjunktiv* |
|---|---|---|
| *ich* | *konnte* | *könnte* |
| *du* | *konntest* | *könntest* |
| *er/sie/es* | *konnte* | *könnte* |
| *wir* | *konnten* | *könnten* |
| *ihr* | *konntet* | *könntet* |
| *sie/Sie* | *konnten* | *könnten* |

Remember, too, that suggestions are also often expressed with the imperative of the verb, acompanied by the particles *doch* and/or *mal*: *Gehen Sie doch mal ins Hofbräuhaus!* (*Schritte international 2*, Chapter 9).

**4**    **Translate into English.**

**a**   *Es ist schon spät. Trotzdem bereitet*

*Lisa noch das Essen für morgen vor.*

.......................................................

.......................................................

**b**   *Nina soll nicht so viel telefonieren. Sie ruft*

*trotzdem jeden Tag ihre Freundinnen an.*

.......................................................

.......................................................

**c**   *Wir würden Sie und Ihre Frau gern*

*zu einem Glas Wein einladen.*

*– Das ist sehr nett von Ihnen, wir*

*kommen gern.*

.......................................................

.......................................................

.......................................................

.......................................................

**d**   *Lara, könnten wir nicht mal wieder*

*zusammen Karten spielen?*

*– Ja, gute Idee. Wie wäre es am Samstag?*

*Könntet ihr da?*

.......................................................

.......................................................

.......................................................

.......................................................

**5**    **Translate into German.**

**a**   Peter and Lena love each other very much.

Despite that, they argue a lot.

.......................................................

.......................................................

**b**   I'm always very tired when I go to bed.

In spite of that, I can't sleep. What should

I do?

– I would go to the doctor.

.......................................................

.......................................................

.......................................................

.......................................................

**c**   This weekend, we could go to the movies

again. Are you interested?

– I would like to go along, but I have

guests.

.......................................................

.......................................................

.......................................................

.......................................................

**d**   We went to Nice and now we're lying

on the beach here. The weather is fantastic!

– How great! We would like to go (be)

there now, too. It's raining here.

.......................................................

.................................................... *klasse!*

*Wie schön!* .........................................

.......................................................

**6**    **Translate into German.**

**a**  What are you going to do on vacation, Ms. Schmidt?

......................................... *machen* ...........................

...................................................................................

– I don't know yet. I'd like to go to Egypt but my husband would rather stay here.

..................... *Ich* ...............................................

...................................................................................

**b**  Are we going on foot or are we taking the car?

........................ *zu Fuß* .........................................

...................................................................................

– I would prefer to go on foot. I sat all day.

......................... *den ganzen Tag* ...........................

**c**  Could you please turn off the radio? I'd like to have a little quiet time.

...................................................................................

.................................................................. *Ruhe.*

– Don't you like music?

......................... *keine* ...........................................

**d**  When I'm done with my studies, I would like to do a master's (degree).

...................................................................................

............................. *einen Master* .........................

– Not me, I'd rather work right away.

...................... *gleich* .............................................

# Listening and Pronunciation

You have already been exposed to syllabic stress and phrase stress as early as Chapters 1–3 of *Schritte international 1*.

In speaking, the accentuation one uses, as well as the pauses one takes, help to produce more specific meaning; in German, this means that the most important information receives the strongest emphasis. This usually appears at the end of a phrase:

*Michael hätte gern ein neues Fahrrad.*
*Ich arbeite viel und komme immer spät nach Hause.*
*Am Wochenende ruhe ich mich aus.*

but it can also appear at the beginning, especially when the sentence begins with a demonstrative pronoun:

*Das hätte er gern.*

# Familiarity and Understanding

## The Grimm Brothers

### Once upon a time ... The origin of the Grimm Brothers' fairy tales

The Grimm brothers did not "invent" the fairy tales which now bear their name; they listened to stories, fables and tales that had been orally passed down for generations and recorded them for posterity in one collection.

Jacob and Wilhelm Grimm, born in Hanau (near Frankfurt) in 1785 and 1786 respectively, were part of a tradition in German scholarship that took root in the early Enlightenment, reaching its height in the late Romantic period, of rediscovering folk traditions as a part of determining what it meant to be "German", since there was no political or historical "Germany" at that time.

While studying at the University of Marburg, the brothers befriended Ludwig Achim von Arnim and Clemens Bretano, whose collection of folk songs titled *Des Knaben Wunderhorn* (The Boy's Magic Horn) in 1805 inspired the Grimms to collect stories from oral traditions, not only to provide a sense of cultural history and identity, but also to preserve the dialects in which the stories were told, particularly by older generations, before those speech patterns disappeared. Though it is commonly believed that they traveled throughout the German-speaking lands transcribing tales told by peasants, in fact most of the stories were told to them by members of their family's circle of friends, people of means who had heard the stories told by their servants. One of their chief informants was a produce seller in their region named Dorothea Viehmann, who had heard many of the tales she shared as a child in her father's inn. Her father was a Hugenot who had been driven from his native France due to religious persecution, and many of the tales he and his customers told were of French origin (such as "*Rotkäppchen*", Little Red Riding Hood), though later research has shown that many of these non-German tales appear in various forms in many cultures.

The first volume of *Kinder- und Hausmärchen* was published around Christmastime in 1812. It contained only 86 fairy tales, but because of the extensive explanatory notes, it was 475 pages long. Though titled *Kindermärchen* (children's fairy tales), the scholarly nature of the book as well as the graphic content of many of the stories led many to deem the tales unsuitable for children. Further volumes and editions followed over the next 25 years, with the 17th edition containing 211 fairy tales. In attempting to increase the audience for the stories (none of the volumes sold well and the Brothers never earned any money from them) changes appeared in several stories to make them more acceptable and appealing, such as Little Red Riding Hood's "liberation" from the wolf's belly (in the original, she did not survive and the story served as a cautionary tale to children to encourage obedience to parents).

**Beyond "Snow White and Rose Red" – The Grimm Brothers' other masterwork**

Though they are best known for and identified with the fairy tales that bear their names, few outside of Germany know of the Grimm Brothers' most ambitious project, the *Deutsches Wörterbuch*.

Jakob and Wilhelm Grimm were professors of philology at the University of Göttingen. Because of their membership in a group of instructors opposed to the new King of Hanover and his authoritarian statutes, they lost their positions at the university. As they were already well known in their field, their former colleagues created a fund in solidarity with them to help the brothers continue their research and thus realize the pursuit of a long-held dream.

Not only were they known for collecting folk tales; the Grimm Brothers had made a name for themselves among linguists for their research into the etymology and grammar of the German language. To complete their work, the brothers wanted to develop a German dictionary encompassing several volumes, which they conceived to describe the historical use of the language from the era of Gutenberg and Luther in the 16th century through the age of Goethe, who died in 1832.
Both brothers set to work on the project in 1838 with the expectation that it would take ten years to complete. Working with 80 collaborators who concentrated their research and documentation on the transformations of words used in historical sources, they compiled over 600,000 pieces of data from the 15th century up to their time.
Of particular interest here is that, unlike many dictionaries of the Enlightenment era which preceded their professional activity, the Grimms did not seek to prescribe proper meaning or usage, but rather to describe how language was actually used and how it changed over time.

The first volume was published in 1854, but the brothers only completed letters A–D by 1859, when Wilhelm Grimm died at the age of 73. His brother Jakob finished the letter F of the fourth volume before passing away in 1863. The entire dictionary would take not the planned ten years, but more than another 100 years to complete. The history of *Grimms Wörterbuch der deutschen Sprache* is full of trials and tribulations, both in terms of its path to completion and in the academic matters involved. In the 1950s, the emergence of two separate German states added another twist in tracing the language's development. The final volume, number 32, of this magnum opus containing 320,000 entries and over 67,000 columns of print in total, was finally published on January 4, 1961.

The entire work is available today as a 33-volume paperback edition from the publisher dtv (Deutscher Taschenbuch Verlag). In order to expand its audience even further, the University of Trier in southwest Germany, through its *Kompetenzzentrum für elektronische Erschließungs- und Publikationsverfahren in den Geisteswissenschaften an der Universität Trier* (Competence Center for Electronic Development and Publication Techniques in the Humanities), undertook to scan this entire linguistic treasure, but with different font sizes and types used throughout, and with special characters used by different contributors, scanning proved to be only part of the process.
The problem was this: how to decrypt 300,000,000 signs, letters, symbols and other data? If the pages were scanned, with 10,000 signs per page and an accuracy rate of 99.9%, there still remained 10 errors per page. How could one manually find those remaining errors? The solution was both simple and effective: two copies of the entire dictionary were typed in China by typists who did not understand the texts they were typing, thus ensuring that they would not be tempted to editorialize. The two copies were then compared, first mechanically and then manually, thereby eliminating most of the errors.

The 33 print volumes are now available on 2 CD-ROMs (MP3). The University of Trier has an online version of the dictionary, but the search functionality required to use the online version is available only on the CD-ROM.

## Wilhelm Hauff

A caliph and his grand vizier fall under the spell of a scheming sorcerer and turn into storks, forced to seek the magic word they had forgotten because they laughed; a little boy is abducted by an old witch, and when he laughs at her nose, she casts a spell that makes him so ugly his own family turns from him in disgust; and in both cases, the stories have happy endings. The stork not only finds the magic word but his true love, and the boy made ugly becomes a master chef, finds the ingredient that will break the spell, and is restored to his own face and family.

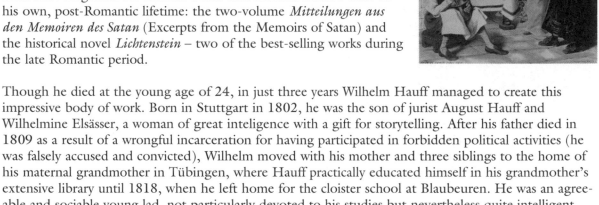

Most German speakers are well acquainted with the tales of Wilhelm Hauff, such as *Kalif Storch* (Caliph Stork), *Zwerg Nase* (Dwarf Longnose), *Der kleine Muck* (Little Mook), *Das Wirtshaus im Spessart* (The Inn in Spessart) or *Das kalte Herz* (Cold Heart), to name some examples. Between 1826 and 1828, Hauff published his three *Märchen-Almanach* volumes, inspired by the *Thousand and One Nights* and Boccacio's *Decamarone*, among other works, one volume each year. They have been translated into numerous languages and have assured Hauff a place in the history of world literature. However, most have forgotten the satirical works that secured Hauff's fame in his own, post-Romantic lifetime: the two-volume *Mitteilungen aus den Memoiren des Satan* (Excerpts from the Memoirs of Satan) and the historical novel *Lichtenstein* – two of the best-selling works during the late Romantic period.

Though he died at the young age of 24, in just three years Wilhelm Hauff managed to create this impressive body of work. Born in Stuttgart in 1802, he was the son of jurist August Hauff and Wilhelmine Elsässer, a woman of great inteligence with a gift for storytelling. After his father died in 1809 as a result of a wrongful incarceration for having participated in forbidden political activities (he was falsely accused and convicted), Wilhelm moved with his mother and three siblings to the home of his maternal grandmother in Tübingen, where Hauff practically educated himself in his grandmother's extensive library until 1818, when he left home for the cloister school at Blaubeuren. He was an agreeable and sociable young lad, not particularly devoted to his studies but nevertheless quite intelligent, with a fantastic imagination and a precocious talent for rhetoric, though he suffered under the separation from his family and never found it easy to adapt to the school's strict discipline.

From 1820 to 1824, he studied theology at the Tübinger Stift, earning his doctorate. Instead of pursuing a career in theology, and thanks to a family member's intercession, he obtained a position as tutor to the children of General Baron Ernst Eugen von Hügel in Stuttgart. In this position, which he held until 1826, and with the support of the Baron's wife, Hauff began crafting and publishing the tales that would make him famous. At the same time, he wrote the satirical works *Mitteilungen aus den Memoiren des Satan* (first part) and *Der Mann im Mond*, the former of which so closely parodied the style of Heinrich Clauren that it was published under a pseudonym closely resembling Clauren: H. Claure. The real Heinrich Clauren (whose own real name was actually Karl Heun) then brought suit against Hauff. Not only did the editor who published the work end up paying damages to Clauren/Heun, but the parody was an enormous success and Hauff then satirized the entire escapade in a short work, *Controvers-Predigt über H. Clauren und den Mann im Monde*, which is considered one of the best examples of the author's ironic, sarcastic style.

In 1826, during a two-year engagement to his cousin Luise Hauff, the young writer embarked on a trip abroad – his *grande tour* –, taking him from Frankfurt to Paris, Normandy, Brussels, Antwerp, Cologne, and then Bremen, Hamburg, Berlin, Leipzig and Dresden before returning to Stuttgart. During the seven months of his voyage, he completed the second half of the *Memoiren des Satan* and other short novels; in Bremen, he suffered unrequited love; in Berlin, he was introduced into literary circles; in Dresden, he was able to visit his idol, Ludwig Tieck; and everywhere he went, he was well received and enjoyed the fine reputation of his published works. In January of 1827, Hauff was named editor of the Cotta publication *Morgenblatt für gebildete Stände*, and in February, he married Luise. Despite the heavy workload of the *Morgenblatt* as well as conflicts with the owner, Hauff continued to pursue his own writing, producing short stories, poetry, newspaper columns and literary criticism, all the while preparing to write another novel. In the summer of 1827, despite feeling unwell, he took a trip to Tyrol to see the original settings of some of his new work. Four weeks after his return to Stuttgart, his condition worsened. On November 18, one week after the birth of his only child, Wilhelm Hauff died of a fever of unspecified origin.

This author's extraordinary output, his popularity and the enormous and lasting success of some of his works, especially his fairy tales, contrast vividly with the indifference and skepticism that some critics have leveled against him, particularly in claims that he only served the fashion of the moment, that he lacked originality and maturity. Other critics, however, have praised his fantastic imagination, his bright and versatile style, the beauty of his texts and their humor and irony, his writing inspired by Jean Paul and E.T.A. Hoffmann, Cervantes and Sir Walter Scott, and comparing him to the Grimm Brothers and Hans Christian Andersen. The early 20th century writer and journalist Kurt Tucholsky, for example, wrote in 1918: *"Wenn jemand bewusst dichtet, Märchen dichtet, … dann ist ein Wunder geschehen. Meines Wissens in der Literatur nur zweimal: bei Andersen und bei Hauff."* (When one consciously writes, writes fairy tales... then a miracle has happened. To my knowledge only twice in literature: in the cases of Andersen and Hauff.)

For nearly two centuries, the general public has enjoyed his stories: alongside innumerable editions and translations, generations of illustrators of literature for young people have created images of Caliph Stork and Dwarf Longnose among others; his stories have been made into numerous films, and in the mid-nineteeth century even inspired Duke Wilhelm of Urach to rebuild the Lichtenstein castle as Hauff had described it in his historical novel. Still, the most lasting legacy is the fact that even into the 21st century, children young and not so young still read, listen to, laugh along with and dream upon the amazing stories of the imaginative, postromantic writer Wilhelm Hauff.

Hans Christian Hagedorn

## Etymology of the days of the week

The Romans gave the days of the week names inspired by seven of their gods – also major heavenly bodies (the sun, moon, Mars, Mercury, Jupiter, Venus and Saturn); those names were then adopted and adapted by the Germanic peoples in the 4th century to reflect their own traditions and interpretations.

**Montag:** As with many idioms, this day's name has its roots in Latin: *dies lunae (Mond* = moon*)*. The German expression *blauer Montag* (blue Monday), meaning to not work on Monday, takes its name from the tradition of decorating churches in blue on the Mondays in Lent. (Nowadays, this tradition is still followed by many hair salons and restaurants in Germany.) The phrase *blaumachen (*"to make blue") takes its meaning in part from this tradition, but is more tied to the medieval process for dying cloth with indigo. In order to keep the dye bath at the proper acidity, large quantities of urine were required, meaning that the workers had to drink sufficiently to keep the vats balanced. In short order, those workers consuming large amounts of beer in the sunshine were good for nothing else, and the tradition was born. To this day, the adjective *blau* also means "drunk" or "inebriated" and not "depressed" as the color indicates in English.

The Monday preceding Mardi Gras and Ash Wednesday is known as *Rosenmontag* in German, taking its name from a tradition involving the Pope presenting a golden rose on the Sunday before Lent (and not from the verb *rasen* [to run, race], referring to the parades that begin on that day).

**Dienstag:** *Martis dies* in Latin refers to Mars Thingsus, the protector of Thing (*Ding* – thing, object). The Germanic god's name was Ziu; speaking linguistically, the name is "descended" from that of the Greek god Zeus.

**Mittwoch:** In many Western languages, this name derives from *dies mercuri*, but the Church, hoping to stamp out more pagan practices, substituted a more generic name signifying the middle of the week (*Mitte der Woche*).

**Donnerstag:** The occurrence of *Donner* in this name comes from the Germanic god Donar, analagous to the Roman Jupiter, also known as Jove. Thus, *Donnerstag* is the Germanic version of *Jovis dies*. The English Thursday then derives from the Norse equivalent of Jove/Donar, Thor.

**Freitag:** The Germanic goddess Freya, Wodan's mate, names the fifth day, as the Roman analogy, Venus, names the day in Latin *(veneris dies)*.

**Samstag, Sonnabend:** There are two names in German for this day; *Samstag*, recognized all over the German-speaking areas, is the only name for the day in the South and in the East; *Sonnabend* is used in the north and in central Germany. *Samstag* has its etymological root in the Hebrew "sabbat" (sabbath), as opposed to *Sonnabend*, which stems from an old Anglicism (Sunday eve), introduced by an 8th century missionary (Boniface) into the Germanic regions as a way to purge both the pagan Roman traditions and the Hebrew influence. Ironically, in England where the Anglican tradition was born, the name of the day, Saturday, is derived from the Latin *saturno dies* (day of Saturn).

**Sonntag:** Sonne (sun), a pagan name with Latin origins, as the Romans counted the sun among the planets and so named a day for it *(dies solis)*. Though German still carries this tradition, in the Romance languages, a more Christian tradition of naming has prevailed (dimanche, domingo, etc.).

## Historical Fragments

### Wilhelm Tell, the Swiss Guard and the Red Cross – Notes on Swiss history

The legendary 14th century Swiss warrior hero Wilhelm Tell was forced to shoot an arrow through an apple placed on his son's head, for the simple reason that the rebel Tell had refused to salute a cap symbolizing the ruler of the House of Austria. Tell was such a good shot that the incident ended without injury.

Legend or not, the poet and playwright Friedrich Schiller used this saga in his drama of the same name, *Wilhelm Tell*, in 1804, as the central event in Switzerland's struggle for freedom. The facts of the founding of Switzerland, however, speak more to the Oath of Rütli (a mountain meadow where the three cantons, Schwyz, Uri and Unterwalden swore eternal union) in 1291. While Schiller's drama focuses on the rights of the Swiss people and human freedoms as Classical and Enlightenment ideals, these three original cantons were actually motivated to form their Confederation in order to promote free trade and protect important trade routes. Because of the Holy Roman Emperor's duty to protect the Pope in Rome, routes through the Alps between Germany, where the Emperors sat, and Italy were key, and the tension surrounding control over these roads lay at the heart of conflict between Switzerland and the larger imperial powers surrounding the cantons for several centuries.

The cantons' first struggle against the Habsburgs began in 1315 and was over quickly; at the battle of Morgarten, an army of peasants defeated the far better armed and trained Habsburg military, and it is said that 2,000 Habsburg troops died, compared to only 12 Swiss peasants. Militarily speaking, this battle was signifcant: an infantry battalion had slain an entire army, which consequently established the renown of the Swiss soldiers. Hence, many Swiss earned their pay as foreign mercenaries until the practice was banned in 1856, with one exception: the Swiss Guard has protected the Pope in the Vatican since 1506.

The struggle against the Habsburgs continued until 1474 when Switzerland was finally recognized as an independent state within the Holy Roman Empire. In 1499, the cantons also became independent of the Holy Roman Empire thanks to their victory in the Swabian War, but there emerged a new concern: Switzerland's desire to secure ports, leading to planned conquests in northern Italy. In 1513, the Swiss, considered militarily invincible at this time, attempted to invade territory ruled by Milan (then under French control) in northern Italy until 1515. But Emperor Francis I of France ended Switzerland's military dominance at the Battle of Marignano in 1515, and until 1815, the Swiss Confederation remained under French influence.

Religious differences between the cantons led to discord. In 1523, the reformer Ulrich Zwingli introduced the Protestant Reformation and a few years later, in 1541, Johannes Calvin (John Calvin) applied his own Calvinist reform that quickly spread throughout Europe. Later, via England and the Netherlands (where they were called "Puritans"), they went to what would become the United States. In France, their followers were called Hugenotten (Huguenots – "Confederates") and were persecuted by King Louis XIV in 1685. 60,000 Huguenots fled to Switzerland and established the watch and textile industries there. Also in Switzerland there was a strong tendency toward frequent conflicts between Catholics and Protestants which lasted until the 18th century.

During the Enlightenment, Zurich became the "Athens of the River Limmat". Many philosophers and educators, influenced by the ideas of Jean-Jacques Rousseau (born in Geneva in 1712), lived and published their works there, including Johann Caspar Lavater (now often considered more opposed to the Enlightenment than a part of it, due to his controversial views on physiognomy) and Johann Heinrich Pestalozzi. A sort of Swiss "tourism" began to take hold among the intelligentsia of Europe.

Later, Napoleon occupied Switzerland and terminated the Confederation's government; Switzerland became a vassal state of France and was forced to send mercenaries to Spain and Russia. The current form of the Swiss Confederation was established in 1848 as a modern federal state. All customs duties were abolished, and each of the cantons combined to create a unified internal market, resulting in substantial economic growth. Thus Switzerland is considered a forerunner of contemporary Europe.

In 1863, the businessman Henry Dunant, shocked by the horrors of the Battle of Solferino in 1859, founded the "International Committee of the Red Cross". Included in the Geneva Convention is the provision that under international law, medics are to be treated as neutral parties in any armed conflict. As a symbol of their services, the Swiss flag is inverted: a red cross appears on a white background.

# Self-Evaluation

**The Weekend**

☺ ☺ ☺

---

### When listening, I can understand (Hören)

– a telephone conversation concerning plans for the weekend
– advice or tips on the radio concering leisure activities: *„Dieses Straßenfest ist inzwischen weit über die Grenzen von Berlin hinaus bekannt.“*
– a short fairy tale such as *„Hans im Glück“*

### In written texts, I can understand (Lesen)

– a note giving advice: *„Schlaf nicht so lange, … telefonier nicht so viel.“*
– an activity program: *Weihnachtsstücke für Klavier und Orchester im Berliner Dom. Studentenermäßigung.*
– press releases on leisure activities
– a glossary with word translations specific to contexts: *Sonntagsbeilage, Sonntagsbraten*
– a survey in a magazine: *Unsere Leserumfrage: „Wochenend' und Sonnenschein“*

### I can produce the following oral structures (Sprechen)

– express contrary notions: *„Nina soll nicht so lange schlafen. Trotzdem bleibt sie bis zehn Uhr im Bett.“*
– express wishes: *„Ich wäre jetzt gern in Berlin. / Ich hätte gern mal ein bisschen Ruhe.“*
– make suggestions: *„Wir könnten mal wieder Karten spielen.“*
– accept or reject suggestions: *„Einverstanden. / Schade, das geht leider nicht. / Ich bin dagegen.“*

### I can produce the following written texts (Schreiben)

– an e-mail to Germany describing my plans for the weekend

| Kursbuch | Textbook |
|---|---|

### Seite 18 | ### page 18

| das Fachgeschäft, -e | specialty shop |
| der Flohmarkt, ⸚e | flea market |
| handeln | to negotiate |
| *die Warenwelt (Sg)* | *the world of goods and wares* |

### Seite 19 | ### page 19

| halten von, du hältst, er hält, er hat gehalten | to think of something or someone (have an opinion) |
| *der Lampion, -s* | *lampion (small lantern)* |
| das Metall, -e | metal |
| die Qualität, -en | quality |

### Seite 20 | ### page 20

| das Besteck, -e | flatware |
| die Kamera, -s | camera |
| das Klassenzimmer, – | classroom |
| *mechanisch* | *mechanical* |
| *die Mütze, -n* | *cap* |
| *der Schal, -s* | *scarf* |
| der Sessel, – | armchair |
| *das Silberbesteck, -e* | *silverware* |
| tief | deep |
| *verschönern* | *to beautify* |
| *die Zuckerdose, -n* | *sugar bowl* |

### Seite 21 | ### page 21

| der Bildschirm, -e | (view) screen |
| die Couch, -s/-en | couch |
| *eckig* | *angular, square-cut* |
| die Eisenbahn, -en | railroad |
| elektrisch | electric |
| die Elektroware, -n | electronic device |
| das Fernsehgerät, -e | television set |
| flach | flat |
| *die Haushaltswaren (Pl)* | *household goods* |
| *die Lokomotive, -n* | *locomotive* |
| *der Milchtopf, ⸚* | *milk pan* |
| die Platte, -n | here: table top |
| *die Sohle, -n* | *sole (of a shoe)* |
| das Spielzeug (Sg) | toy |
| der Stoff, -e | fabric, cloth |
| *das Topf-Set, -s* | *cookware set* |
| Verzeihung | here: forgive me |

### Seite 22 | ### page 22

| *die Auswahl (Sg)* | *selection* |
| bequem | comfortable |
| *der Deckel, –* | *lid* |
| *der Deckelöffner, –* | *jar or bottle opener* |
| *die Gemüsereibe, -n* | *vegetable grater* |
| *gründlich* | *here: thoroughly* |
| die Haut (Sg) | skin |
| *der Jahrmarkt, ⸚e* | *annual fair, carnival* |
| *die Karotte, -n* | *carrot* |
| *der Ohrring, -e* | *earring* |
| *reiben, er hat gerieben* | *here: to grate* |
| reinigen | to clean |
| *die Reisetasche, -n* | *travel bag* |
| der Strumpf, ⸚e | stocking, hose |
| das Tuch, ⸚er | cloth, scarf |
| *das Wunderputztuch, ⸚er* | *miracle cleaning cloth* |
| *zu·greifen, er hat zugegriffen* | *to dig in, help oneself* |

### Seite 23 | ### page 23

| *alkoholisch* | *alcoholic, containing alcohol* |
| auf·nehmen, du nimmst auf, er nimmt auf, er hat aufgenommen | here: to take out |
| das Gas (Sg) | gas (natural gas) |
| *das Haushaltsgerät, -e* | *household appliance* |
| die Kommunikation, -en | communication |
| *die Konsumausgabe, -n* | *consumer spending* |
| der Kredit, -e | loan, line of credit |
| *monatlich* | *monthly* |
| *die Musikanlage, -n* | *music system* |
| das Nahrungsmittel, – | nourishment |
| *der Tabak, -e* | *tabacco* |
| wert sein | to be valuable |

### Seite 24 | ### page 24

| damals | then, back then |
| *der Drache, -n* | *dragon* |
| *die Einleitung, -en* | *introduction* |
| die Erinnerung, -en | memory |
| der Gegenstand, ⸚e | object |
| *der Harlekin, -e* | *harlequin* |
| *nach·gucken* | *to see, peek* |
| *der Plastikdrache, -n* | *dragon sculpture, figure* |
| *das Porzellan (Sg)* | *porcelain* |
| *die Porzellanpuppe, -en* | *porcelain doll* |
| *die Probe, -n* | *here: rehearsal* |
| *der Regisseur, -e* | *director* |
| *der Theaterregisseur, -e* | *director (of stage)* |
| die Überschrift, -en | text heading |

| | |
|---|---|
| um Himmels Willen | for Heaven's sake |
| unhöflich | impolite |
| wertvoll | valuable |

## Seite 25 — page 25

| | |
|---|---|
| die Adjektivdeklination, -en | adjective declension |
| die Äußerung, -en | statement, utterance |
| ein·leiten | to introduce, preface |
| der unbestimmte Artikel, – | indefinite article |
| der Vergleichspartikel, – | comparison particle |

## Seite 26 — page 26

| | |
|---|---|
| bewegt | moved, emotional |
| die Bluesmusik (Sg) | blues music |
| China (Sg) | China |
| die Countrymusik (Sg) | country music |
| die Erfindung, -en | invention |
| exportieren | to export |
| die Grundidee, -n | basic idea |
| die Hosentasche, -n | pants pocket, trouser pocket |
| melancholisch | melancholy |
| die Milliarde, -n | billion |
| die Million, -en | million |
| miteinander | with each other |
| der MP3-Player, – | MP3 player |
| die Mundharmonika, -s | harmonica, blues harp |
| die Mundharmonika-Gruppe, -n | harmonica group, band |
| musikalisch | musical |
| das Musikinstrument, -e | musical instrument |
| die Popkultur (Sg) | popular culture |
| produzieren | to produce |
| rund um | all around |
| die Single, -s | single |
| verantwortlich sein | to be responsible |
| das Weihnachtslied, -er | Christmas song |
| württembergisch | from the Württemberg region |

## Seite 27 — page 27

| | |
|---|---|
| erfinden, er hat erfunden | to invent |
| der Füller, – | fountain pen |
| das Kürbiskernöl, -e | pumpkin seed oil |
| der Lehrplan, ̈e | lesson plan |
| das Raumschiff, -e | spaceship |
| recherchieren | to research |

## Arbeitsbuch — Workbook

## Seite 92 — page 92

| | |
|---|---|
| das Bein, -e | leg |
| die Halskette, -n | necklace |
| rein·passen | to fit (into something or somewhere) |

## Seite 93 — page 93

| | |
|---|---|
| der Einkaufszettel, – | shopping list |

## Seite 94 — page 94

| | |
|---|---|
| die Endung, -en | ending |
| der Händler, – | trader |

## Seite 95 — page 95

| | |
|---|---|
| jmdm. auf den Wecker gehen | to get on someone's nerves |

## Seite 96 — page 96

| | |
|---|---|
| der Angebotsprospekt, -e | brochure detailing offerings available |
| die Bildschirmgröße, -n | viewscreen size |
| das Hochhaus, ̈er | high-rise building |
| das Pferd, -e | horse |
| die Tiefe, -n | depth |

## Seite 98 — page 98

| | |
|---|---|
| die Urlaubsreise, -n | vacation trip |

## Seite 99 — page 99

| | |
|---|---|
| begleiten | to accompany |
| der Kinderschuh, -e | child's shoe |

## 1    Adjective declension: indefinite article
### *(Adjektivdeklination: unbestimmter Artikel)*

| examples | nominative | |
|---|---|---|
| **m** | *Das ist aber **ein schöner Ring**!*<br>*– Ja, der ist schön.* | My but that's a beautiful ring!<br>– Yes, it is beautiful. |
| **n** | *Das ist aber **ein originelles Foto**!*<br>*– Ja, es ist originell.* | Isn't that an original photograph!<br>– Yes, it is original. |
| **f** | *Da ist **eine billige Lampe**.*<br>*– Ja, die ist billig.* | There's a cheap lamp.<br>– Yes, it is cheap. |
| **pl** | *Hier sind **interessante Bücher**.*<br>*– Ja, die sind wirklich interessant.* | Here are interesting books.<br>– Yes, they're really interesting. |

As we have seen before and in contrast to English, adjectives that precede nouns (attributive adjectives) always take endings in German:
*Das ist ein schöner Ring.*

Again, adjectives that are separated from the noun (predicate adjectives) do not change form:
*Der Ring ist schön.*

When an adjective is attributive and precedes the noun, there must be an indication of the noun's gender, case and/or number. In other words, within the entire noun phrase, the reader or listener must be able to tell whether the noun is masculine, feminine, or neuter; what case the noun is in; and whether it is singular or plural. If the noun's article does not give that information, the adjective ending must do so.
Thus, if a noun is preceded by *ein*, it is impossible to tell just from the article whether the noun is masculine or neuter. The adjective ending then does this:
*ein schöner Ring*
*ein originelles Foto*

Though a definite article will always give that information, an indefinite article, particularly in the nominative case, often does not.

The negative article (*kein, keine*) functions in the same way as *ein/eine*. Here, though, there is the added aspect of plural. Because *keine* and the noun form already tell the listener or reader that it is plural, the ending for any plural adjective in any case, whenever there is any article at all, is *-en*:
*Das sind **keine** interessanten Bücher.*

Compare:

| | |
|---|---|
| **m** | *ein / kein schöner Ring* |
| **n** | *ein / kein originelles Foto* |
| **f** | *eine / keine günstige Lampe* |
| **pl** | *– interessante / keine interessanten Bücher* |

| examples | | accusative | |
|---|---|---|---|
| | m | *Ich habe einen schönen Ring gekauft.* | I bought a beautiful ring. |
| | n | *Wir möchten ein originelles Foto.* | We would like an original photograph. |
| | f | *Haben Sie eine billige Lampe?* | Do you have an inexpensive lamp? |
| | pl | *Ralph findet immer interessante Bücher.* | Ralph always finds interesting books. |

The only difference in forms between nominative and accusative case is the masculine, and here the adjective ending, just like the articles, is *-en*.

| examples | | dative | |
|---|---|---|---|
| | m | *Wir sind heute bei einem guten Freund eingeladen.* | Today, we were invited to the home of a good friend. |
| | n | *Ich kaufe den Computer lieber in einem anderen Geschäft.* | I prefer to buy the computer in another store. |
| | f | *Bei einer neuen Lampe hast du Garantie.* | With a new lamp, you have a guarantee. |
| | pl | *Ich möchte eine Wohnung mit hellen Zimmern.* | I would like an apartment with bright rooms. |

As you see in these examples, all adjectives in dative case end in *-en*. When you consider that the articles always show the gender and case, it makes sense. Furthermore, the plural definite article, *den*, is reflected even when there is no article.

## 2   Comparison *(Komparation)*

| examples | *Der Rock ist aber **schön**!* | My but that dress is beautiful! |
|---|---|---|
| | *– Ich finde den hier **schöner**.* | – I find this one here more beautiful. |
| | *Nein, der rote hier, der ist **am schönsten**.* | No, the red one here, it's the most beautiful. |

Comparative forms in German follow a pattern very similar to the English pattern. However, while English only uses the endings -er and -est for some adjectives and adverbs, mostly single-syllable, German uses these endings for all adjectives and adverbs, regardless of the length of the word. There is no literal German equivalent for "more x" and "most x"; it is <u>always</u> -er and -(e)st, with an adjective ending if needed.

Superlative forms in the predicate, such as in the final example, require the particle *am* and the ending expands to *-sten*.

| examples | *Lisas Wohnung ist **groß**.* | Lisa's apartment is large. |
|---|---|---|
| | *– Die von Anne ist **größer**.* | – Anne's is larger. |
| | ***Am größten** ist die von Petra.* | The largest is Petra's. |

In the case of single-syllable adjectives, the vowels *a*, *o* and *u*, often umlaut to *ä*, *ö* and *ü*:
*alt – älter – am ältesten*
*groß – größer – am größten*
*jung – jünger – am jüngsten*

In *Schritte international 2*, Chapter 13, we already came across the most common exceptions:
*gut – besser – am besten*
*viel – mehr – am meisten*
*gern – lieber – am liebsten*

## 3 Comparison particles: *als, wie (Vergleichspartikel: „als, wie")*

examples | *Ich finde die Kette **schöner als** die Ohrringe.* | I think the necklace is prettier than the earrings.
*Pedro wohnt **weiter** entfernt **als** Mario.* | Pedro lives farther away than Mario (does).

When comparing one object to another, the second object is preceded by **als**.

examples | *Ich finde die Kette **genauso schön wie** die Ohrringe.* | I think the necklace is just as pretty as the earrings.
*Pedro wohnt **genauso weit** entfernt **wie** Mario.* | Pedro lives exactly as far away as Mario (does).

When comparing two equal objects, the adjective is preceded by *genauso* and the second element of the comparison is introduced with the particle *wie*. The adjective remains in the base (positive) form.

## 4 Translate into English.

**a** *Der Schal ist schön, oder?* ......................................................................

*– Hm, ich weiß nicht, ich finde diesen hier* ......................................................................

*schöner.* ......................................................................

**b** *Wie findest du die Reisetasche?* ......................................................................

*– Nicht schlecht, aber ein Koffer ist* ......................................................................

*praktischer.* ......................................................................

**c** *Wie findest du diese Kaffeekanne?* ......................................................................

*– Hm, ich finde sie ein bisschen zu groß.* ......................................................................

*Möchtest du nicht lieber eine kleinere* ......................................................................

*Kaffeekanne?* ......................................................................

**d** *Sieh mal die Schuhe an!* ......................................................................

*– Sie sind aber sehr teuer. Kauf lieber* ......................................................................

*billigere Schuhe.* ......................................................................

**5**    **Translate into English.**

**a**   *Ich habe dir etwas mitgebracht.* ....................................................................................

    *– Was denn?* ....................................................................................

    *Fußballschuhe.* ....................................................................................

    *– Oh, die sind genial!* ....................................................................................

**b**   *Wofür geben Sie das meiste Geld aus?* ...............................................................................?

    *– Ich kaufe gern Kleidung, aber am meisten* ....................................................................................

    *gebe ich für Urlaub aus.* ....................................................................................

**c**   *Entschuldigung, wo kann man hier billig* ....................................................................................

    *essen?* ....................................................................................

    *– Am billigsten ist die Pizzeria „Verdi".* ....................................................................................

**d**   *Kann ich Ihnen helfen?* ....................................................................................

    *– Ja, bitte. Ich suche einen dunklen Anzug* ....................................................................................

    *mit einem eleganten Jackett.* ....................................................................................

**6**    **Translate into English.**

**a**   What do you think of these shoes? ....................................................................................

    – Aren't they too lightweight? ....................................................................................

    No, right now I'm looking for lightweight ....................................................................................

    shoes! ....................................................................................

**b**   Oh, what's that? ............................................................. *denn*

    – Those are old books. I found them at the ..................................................... *auf dem*

    flea market. ....................................................................................

**c**   Look, there's a black jacket. ..................... *mal* ...............................................

    – Yeah, but I don't need a black jacket, ....................................................................................

    I'd like a brown jacket. ....................................................................................

**d**   Can I help you? ............................................ *Ihnen* .........................

    – Yes, please. I'm looking for a long skirt ....................................................................................

    made of lightweight material. *aus* ........................................................................

## 7 Translate into German.

**a** This is a very good cell phone.

....................................................

– Yes, but I like this one here better.

................ *das hier* ...........................

**b** I like the green necklace better than the

........................................ *mir besser* ........

blue earrings.

....................................................

– Yes, but the carrings are cheaper.

....................................................

**c** Today is nicer weather than yesterday.

*Heute ist* ..........................................

– Yeah, we could have a little excursion,

....................................................

don't you think?

....................................................

**d** What do you spend more money on, (on)

....................................................

the car or (on) clothes?

....................................................

– We spend just as much money on the

*Für* ...............................................

car as on clothes.

....................................................

# Listening and Pronunciation

In most spoken utterances in German, the word in the final position of a phrase gets the primary emphasis, as it also tends to be the most relevant to the information being imparted.
Practice the difference between the principal stress within each word (which syllable gets the emphasis within the word, „´") and the phrase stress, where the most relevant word is stressed more than the others. This subtle difference often rests upon the length of time a word is spoken more than the volume.

*ein dícker wármer <u>Schal</u>*
*von eínem álten <u>Freund</u>*

# Familiarity and Understanding

### Calling them by name

Hearing the names *Siemens, Daimler, Porsche, Bosch, Benz* or *Beiersdorf* likely triggers thoughts of large German multinational conglomerates. These names also share one other common element: in the beginning of each company, there was an inventor by that name who was able to exploit his idea to create a new business.

Though the inventor of the first affordable car back in the 1920s was an Austrian named *Béla Barényi* (as determined during a legal proceeding in the 1950s), the most famous inventor was *Ferdinand Porsche* who came up with the Volkswagen *Käfer* (the original Beetle). Less well known is the fact that Porsche also developed the first hybrid car in the early part of the 20th century. At the Paris World's Fair in 1900, it was unveiled with an engine powered by batteries built ito the wheel wells, a model employed 70 years later by NASA in the design of the lunar rover.

*Paul Carl Beiersdorf* was a pharmacist whose patent on medical plasters in 1882 is considered the founding of the company that today makes Nivea, Eucerin and numerous other well-known brands.

Such is also the case with *Werner von Siemens* (1816–1892), who originally trained as an elementary school teacher because his parents could not afford to send him to university, but then enlisted in the army to pursue engineering training. He invented an electroplating process, another process for the insulation of electric cable, and he improved upon existing telegraph technology to outfit the telegraph with a needle which pointed to the correct letter instead of sounding out Morse code. With this development, he founded his first company, which concentrated on building the wire connections, first within Germany and then across Europe and in the 1870s, even from London to Calcutta via Teheran. The Siemens wires eventually encompassed over 11,000 km (6800 miles) of cable.

Later in the 19th century, the company expanded to manufacture locomotives, trams, elevators and other machinery. The company, which began with two men, now employs over 430,000 people worldwide, only 130,000 of whom work in Germany. In addition to transportation and communication, Siemens is also active in medical technology (Werner helped Wilhelm Conrad Röntgen develop the tubes that allowed him to investigate x-rays), lighting, energy and consumer products.

The name *Gottfried Daimler* (1834–1900) is inextricably linked with the auto manufacturer. He invented the internal combustion engine that runs on gasoline and which allowed a vehicle to achieve any real speed. The first vehicle equipped with this engine, in 1885, reached a whopping 12 km (7.5 miles) per hour. A few months later, he outfitted a boat with the same engine, and one year later a four-wheeled carriage. Gottlieb Daimler thus invented the first car.

*Karl Benz* (1844–1929), a contemporary of Daimler, invented the four stroke cycle engine and other essential engine elements such as the spark plug, clutch and carburetor. Benz patented a motorized three-wheeled vehicle which enjoyed as much success as Daimler's four-wheeled version. Though gasoline was not readily available everywhere at that time, the press predicted that his horseless carriage would do well in the future for tourism and business trips. Daimler and Benz never met; Benz & Cie. and Daimler Motor Gesellschaft competed directly with each other until 1926, three years before Benz's death and 26 after Daimler's passing, when their two companies merged to form Daimler-Benz, known today as Daimler AG and employing over 270,000 worldwide, manufacturing over one million cars and nearly half a million trucks annually.

### Enforcing order upon chaos – The German Institute for Standardization

In North America, business letters are written on what is called letter-sized paper. The rest of the world, however, writes their letters on a paper size known as DIN A4. Other than the dimensions, why the different name?
A German golfer recently submited an application for standardization of the weight, size, number and dimples and specifications of flight for a golf ball. Why would he submit this and to whom? Toothbrush bristles must withstand a tensile force of more than 1.5 kg; who set this standard? Especially beyond North America, the size of paper sheets, indeed, the specifications of any manufactured product are set according to internationally recognized standards which really made global industrialization possible; after all, if male and female plugs don't match, what good are they?

The *Deutsches Institut für Normung* (German Institute of Standardization), located in Berlin, is a German institution with a nearly one-hundred-year history (established in 1917) that currently publishes about 2,400 standards per year thanks to the work of over 26,000 expert collaborators. The DIN is the German member of the ISO (International Organization for Standardization), and over 90% of DIN standards are globally recognized through the ISO. The first standard that the DIN established was for a cone form, then named *DIN 1*. In 1922, the Institute described and established standards of paper sizes such as the A4, which are still used today.

The DIN is a private organization funded by its over 1900 members whose dues finance about 8% of the total budget. The remainder is financed by publishing and other business activities (22%) and the sales of its standards (about 52%) with the balance funded by projects linked to industry. Its current budget is about EUR 62,000,000 per year.

The mission of the *Deutsches Institut für Normung* is to develop consensus-based standards which facilitate cost-effective research and development, manufacturing, and business development. Much like the metric system, the adoption of international standards also simplifies life for individuals. Exit signs, for example, look the same in most countries, conforming to DIN/ISO 7000. (U.S. exit signage does not conform to this standard.) The exact layout of business letters on letterhead, both small-sized and enlarged, is laid out line by line, avoiding all confusion (DIN 5008). High-speed rails are safer because the metal used meets a specific standard of heat and cold tolerance. Road surfaces are safer because the asphalt meets standards to avoid water build-up in heavy rains, minimizing aquaplaning; even sports gear is safer because of the standards established for the materials in their manufacture. A company achieving ISO 9001 certification is recognized worldwide as incorporating the highest levels of safety and quality. Not only do such rules protect life and property, but they also enable new companies to enter the global market on a more equitable playing field. These standards thus function as a common language for safety and security in a global market.

In 2007, DIN called for standarization on inclusion in Unicode (letter/character encoding) of an upper-case "ß" which to date had only existed in lower case. Thus, the expression *IN MASSEN*, written in all caps, can no longer mean "in masses" and "in moderation", the "ß" can be included to differentiate. Thus, even matters of less-than-life-or-death importance can be simplified.

### *Gartenzwerge*/Gnomes

The word *Kitsch*, though German, is of nebulous origin; ostensibly, it can be traced back to archaic colloquial use and somehow derived from a common root with the verbs *streichen* and *schmieren* (stroke, smear). In its modern form, it is onomatopoeic; the sound is as unpleasing in English as it is in German. Some have asserted that the word is of Yiddish origin, signifying "giving something to someone that is not at all necessary". In any event, there is no record of the word in written texts before the second half of the 19th century.

This word has made its way into English, French and Spanish to describe mass produced, tasteless, unrefined objects. For many, the perfect example of German *Kitsch* is the ubiquitous *Gartenzwerg*, the ceramic gnomes found in many German gardens.

Reliable estimates claim that more than 25 million of them populate the gardens of Germany, Austria and Switzerland, carrying pickaxes, torches, and tools, pushing wheelbarrows, wearing their work clothes; always smiling, always working, almost always male, sometimes accompanied by a fairy godmother. They are practically an icon of German culture, yet younger generations are losing interest in this forefather of the Smurf.

### The ultimate gift for egg lovers

Many Germans enjoy boiled eggs, hard or soft, on Sunday mornings (or on any morning at hotel breakfast buffets).
For many, that egg heralds the arrival of Sunday. Yet they are divided in one crucial aspect: how to crack the egg. One group believes the egg must be struck gently with the knife or spoon, breaking the shell bit by bit, while the other group simply lops off the egg top in one fell swoop. Freudian interpretations aside, this cultural divide has led to one of the most useless inventions in recent memory with one of the most memorable and least appealing names ever: *der Eiersollbruchstellenverursacher*!
Breaking down this obscenely compound noun, we find 5 or 7 elements, depending on how one looks at it. The translation, literally: "the eggs should break places causer". One clack! and the eggshell cracks exactly where it should.
How it works: a small metal cap is set atop the egg; a ball falls along a metal tube toward the egg and, clack! A circular break appears around the shell where the knife can then pass through to open the egg! *Guten Appetit!*

Promotional brochures describe the *Eiersollbruchstellenverursacher* as a lifestyle article and a great gift idea, making breakfast more fun. Perhaps if it came to America, it could be marketed as the "Egg Clapper"...

### German musical tradition and culture: The seventies and beyond

In *Schritte international 3* Glossary XXL we began a journey into the tradition of German popular music that took us up to the 1960s. In the 40-odd years since, other names and styles have emerged, some of which have already become classics.

### *Krautrock* and *Neue Deutsche Welle*

In the late sixties, popular music from the U.S. and Britain was imitated around the world. Thus, English became the de facto language of music and its fans (though it bears remembering that the Beatles got their professional start in Germany!)

In this atmosphere, a genre of rock music of the seventies emerged, strongly influenced by psychedelic rock and new technologies, called *Krautrock*. Representatives of this genre are *Tangerine Dream*, best known in the U.S. for their soundtrack of the film *Risky Business*, and the oft-admired pioneers *Kraftwerk* with their revolutionary industrial and electronic sound.

The next big scene came in the eighties with the advent of *Neue deutsche Welle* (New German Wave). It consisted of "underground" groups and singers opposed to English language dominance, who sought to create modern songs in their own language. Groups such as *Ideal, Extrabreit, Nena, Rheingold, Trio* and *Münchner Freiheit* or singers such as *Nina Hagen* are the best-known representatives of this movement.

With these postmodern tendencies, many of these groups experienced success across Europe and even into the U.S. and Britain, though their greatest successes came only when their songs were translated into English, such as *Nena* with *99 Luftballons* in 1983 which became 99 Red Balloons, or the Austrian singer *Falco* who had a hit himself with *Amadeus* while his giant hit *Der Kommissar* only achieved mass U.S. acclaim when the band *After the Fire* recorded the song in English translation.

Other German groups, singing only in English, became world famous, such as the *Scorpions* and *Alphaville*. But singing in German is still in fashion, and in the nineties, many well-known groups sang in their mother tongue: *die Prinzen,* for example, bring biting humor to their a capella pop sensibilities, while *die Ärzte, die Toten Hosen* and the pioneering *die Fantastischen Vier*, the first ones to rap in German, also have scored major successes. (It is worth noting that *die Prinzen's* "Ich kann nicht rappen", while not hip-hop, is a splendidly ironic take on the genre.) All have become classic purveyors of modern German music.

### The music scene today: richness and new genres

The effects of the German music surge in the 1990s reach so far that in the 21st century, there is a so-called *Neue Neue Deutsche Welle* (new new German wave).
It is a far more pronounced trend than that of the eighties, encompassing far more singers and groups performing in German, and in more styles. Their success is not only among German-speaking youth. Their riffs are heard constantly on the radio, on cable channels such as VIVA and MTV and on national award programs such as ECHO and COMET.
Obviously, the controversial "quota" helps this; media are required to air at least 30% German music content.

The group *Juli*, offering young fresh pop, captivates audiences. *Silbermond* is considered more "original" with catchy riffs, the guy-friendly *Sportfreunde Stiller* draws legions of fans from the world of *Fußball*, scoring hits with songs of past World Cup victories and providing the soundtrack for a World Cup video game. The group *Wir sind Helden* is a favorite among university students with its brainy lyrics.

The duo *Rosenstolz,* with its swave pop, creates its own unique style, while *Element of Crime* incorporates more jazz elements. Goth and metal fans follow the likes of *Oomph!* or *Rammstein*. The latter has gained a cult following worldwide for their spectacular concerts, including pyrotechnics so intense that the band and audience members often suffer burns.

While *hip hop* originated in depressed neighborhoods of large U.S. cities and expressed their particular social problems, it has also enjoyed astonishing success in the German-speaking countries. *Fettes Brot*, for example, established itself in the mid-90s with its hit *Jein*, while the group *Freundeskreis* delivers political rap.

The future of German music has both tremendous prospects and a high degree of uncertainty. Mulitcultural society and commercial legislation make the scene more colorful and rich, but above all, more settled. Still, as the group *Tokio Hotel* continues to prove there is a place around the world for German bands to find success, if their litany of music awards and disc sales is any indication.

Dolores Rodríguez Cemillán

## Historical Fragments

### Gutenberg, Columbus and the publishing industry

In 1999, the editors of Time Magazine chose Johannes Gutenberg (ca. 1400 – 1468) as the "Man of the Millenium". In 1450, he invented the movable-type printing press in the city of Mainz. His breakthrough was essentially a succession of inventions: first the metal casts for the letters, the process for ordering the letters, and finally a system for maintaining the letters' placement and storage, not to mention modification of existing inks to be able to adhere to the metal type and transfer to the paper. Thus Gutenberg invented the art of printing books using movable type, substantially improving processes that had gone before. Henceforth, not only was an essentially unlimited number of books and formats to become possible, but the prohibitive cost of books would suddenly drop by a factor of thirty. Making the revolution even more appealing to skeptics of the time, Gutenberg's printed materials closely resembled valuable ancient manuscripts.

Such was the manner in which the Gutenberg Bible of 1456 was printed, with an initial run of 150 copies. This first run won over the Pope and the Church, particularly the Benedictines, who for centuries had been preserving the writings of Antiquity by hand copying the classics in their monasteries. And so came about the new opportunity for the Church to publish.

At first, the residents of Mainz guarded the secret of the "divina ars imprimendi" – the divine art of printing. But when enemy troups conquered Mainz in 1462, printers fled to establish new businesses first along the Rhine and then in other areas of Germany, and finally throughout Europe. Presses quickly appeared in Cologne, Basel, Augsburg, Nuremberg, Ulm, Leipzig, Prague and Lübeck. In Paris, then the scientific capital of the world, printers from Mainz opened a bookstore.

The popes invited German printers to Italy, and by the time the first book was published in Venice in 1482, forty printers were established there. German

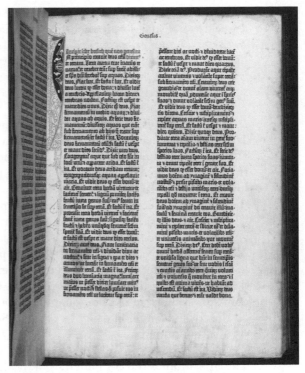

printers established business all over Europe: Johannes de Spira in Venice in 1469, Matthias von Olmütz in Genoa in 1474, Johannes Heynlein – rector of the Sorbonne – in Paris in 1469, and Johann Snell printed Denmark's first book in Odense in 1482 and the first Swedish book one year later. Meanwhile, indigenous publishers sprang up in England, Spain and Portugal.

Because of its importance in the struggle against Muslim encroachment, printing of Christian literature in Spain was considered critical. One well-known book merchant at the time was Christopher Columbus. Having left Portugal in 1484 and entering the service of the Catholic monarchs of Spain in 1486, much of his travel was supported by book sales.

With the arrival of the 16th century, there were 260 printing companies in Europe, publishing about 40,000 texts and books with about 6 million print runs. During the Reformation, the printing industry took on a new urgency in its ability to rapidly reproduce and disseminate the many pamphlets and leaflets the Reformers wrote. Martin Luther's texts in particular were spread with astonishing alacrity, and the first edition of his New Testament in 1522, with an initial printing of 5000 copies, was sold out in three months. By the time of Luther's death in 1546, over 100,000 copies of his Bible were printed. It is estimated that Luther's texts accounted for nearly one-third of all publications in the 16th century.

One major positive side effect of all this printing was the rise in literacy among the general population and even a revolution in education. The availability of material awoke a true hunger for reading. The first German grammar was published in 1534 by Valentin Ickelsamer, who also opened a school in Rothenburg ob der Tauber shortly thereafter. Adam Ries published a basic textbook on mathematics in 1518 while operating *Rechenschulen* (math schools) in Erfurt. (Schooling was not "officially" introduced in Prussia until 1713.)

Another consequence of the proliferation of Luther's writings and his Bible was the starting point for modern High German. In translating the New Testament for German speakers, Luther took great care to phrase the text in such a way that the greatest number could understand it, regardless of dialect. This provided then a baseline, so to speak, for a standard of the language.

The advent of printing also paved the way for the development of newspapers. The first newspaper was a weekly published in the then-free imperial city of Strasburg (in Alsace), titled *Relation aller Fürnemmen und gedenckwürdigen Historien*. Though it was clearly in the German language, and Alsace has often been considered German territory, the first newspaper to definitely be printed in Germany was the "*Aviso*" published in Augsburg in 1609. Around 1650, a Leipzig newspaper began appearing six times per week.

In other countries, the first Dutch newspaper appeared in 1618, followed by a Belgian newspaper in 1620 and in other northern and eastern European countries in ensuing years. Gutenberg's invention was the sole technology for 350 years, producing all books and periodicals until the 19th century, when the iron plate press was invented in 1800, then the typesetter appeared between 1822 and 1884 followed by the rotary press in 1848. These advances, together with improvements in transportation and the abolition of censorship, allowed true mass production and dissemination of books and periodicals. The apex of journalism came in the 1920s in Germany, when over 37,000 newspapers with a total circulation of 25 million were in press. The advent of radio, together the the oppressive policies of the Nazi regime, wiped out this amazing and prodigious industry, and even the Allied victory over fascism in 1945 could not fully resurrect it. The rise of television after World War II eroded the position of daily journalism still further. Nevertheless, Germany is still the largest market in Western Europe for daily newspapers; in the first quarter of 2008, the German Association of Newspaper Publishers reported that over 17 million daily, weekly and Sunday newspapers were sold in Germany, 65% of which were on a subscription basis.

The invention of the computer again revolutionized the entire publishing industry. Whereas layout had been digitally organized, now the entire publishing process is done by computer. The electronic or "e-book" format is already spreading. Though Gutenberg's millenium might seem to be drawing to a close, there is still a devotion to the printed word, leaving his legacy intact for now.

## Self-Evaluation

### The World of Wares

#### When listening, I can understand (Hören)

– statements regarding the location of specific products in a supermarket
– interviews: „*Wofür geben Sie Ihr Geld aus?*" – „*Also, am meisten gebe ich sicher für meine Miete aus.*"

#### In written texts, I can understand (Lesen)

– a statistical graphic concerning consumption in Germany: *Wofür wir am meisten Geld ausgeben.*
– texts on things I like or dislike: *Mein Lieblingsgegenstand. Drei von meinen Sachen.*
– texts on the history of certain instruments: *Rund um die Welt – Mundharmonika (Zwischenspiel)*

#### I can produce the following oral structures (Sprechen)

– offer my opinion: „*Ein braunes Sofa? Das passt doch nicht zu einem Schrank mit schwarzen Türen.*"
– compare some objects to others: „*Ich finde die Kette schöner als die Ohrringe.*" / „*Ein neuer Computer ist mir genauso wichtig wie eine neue Musikanlage.*"
– talk about certain aspects: „*Die Kette habe ich von meinem Freund bekommen. Ich finde sie schön, weil …*"

#### I can produce the following written texts (Schreiben)

– a short text on something I really like: „*Also mein Lieblingsgegenstand ist …*"

| Kursbuch | Textbook |
|---|---|

### Seite 28 — page 28

| | |
|---|---|
| *der Aufkleber, –* | *sticker, adhesive label* |
| *der Karton, -s* | *carton* |
| *der Kuckuck, -e* | *cuckoo* |
| *die Kuckucksuhr, -en* | *cuckoo clock* |
| das Päckchen, – | small package, parcel |
| *verpacken* | *to pack (for shipment)* |
| wiegen, er hat gewogen | to weigh |

### Seite 29 — page 29

| | |
|---|---|
| *die Hörgeschichte, -n* | *story to listen to* |

### Seite 30 — page 30

| | |
|---|---|
| *die Briefsendung, -en* | *sending of a letter* |
| *ein·werfen, du wirfst ein, er wirft ein, er hat eingeworfen* | *to toss in* |
| *jährlich* | *annually* |
| *das Kommunikationsmittel, –* | *means of communication* |
| *die Kursstatistik, -en* | *course/class statistic* |
| *die Kurzmitteilung, -en* | *short message* |
| *leeren* | *to empty* |
| nützen | to use |
| *das Passiv (Sg)* | *passive voice* |
| *per* | *via* |
| *rein·schreiben, er hat reingeschrieben* | *to write in, fill in* |
| sortieren | to sort |
| *die Technologie, -n* | *technology* |
| transportieren | to transport |

### Seite 31 — page 31

| | |
|---|---|
| an·klicken | to click on |
| besorgen | to acquire, get |
| *die Bürokommunikation (Sg)* | *office communication* |
| *digital* | *digital* |
| *die Handtasche, -n* | *handbag, purse* |
| *die Handytasche, -n* | *cell phone purse* |
| *der Katalog, -e* | *catalogue* |
| kriegen | to get |
| *die Langeweile (Sg)* | *boredom* |
| *multifunktional* | *multifunctional* |
| *der Streifen, –* | *stripe* |
| der Vertrag, ¨e | contract |

### Seite 32 — page 32

| | |
|---|---|
| beantragen | to apply for (something to be issued) |
| dabei sein | to be there |

| | |
|---|---|
| egal sein | to be all the same/no difference |
| die Grippeimpfung, -en | influenza vaccination |
| das Konsulat, -e | consulate |
| langweilen (sich) | to bore (be bored) |
| *das Redemittel, –* | *words and phrases for speaking* |
| die Reinigung, -en | here: dry cleaning shop |
| der Schnupfen (Sg) | sniffle |
| die Untersuchung, -en | (medical) examination |
| verabredet sein | to have an appointment |
| verlängern | to extend |
| versprechen, du versprichst, er verspricht, er hat versprochen | to promise |
| *das Visum, Visa* | *visa* |
| vor·kommen, es ist vorgekommen | to occur, happen |
| was für ein/e | what kind of |

### Seite 33 — page 33

| | |
|---|---|
| angenehm | pleasant |
| *an·schalten* | *to turn on, switch on* |
| die Bahn, -en | railroad |
| die Geburtstagsfeier, -n | birthday party |
| *genervt* | *annoyed, aggravated* |
| *gut·tun, es hat gutgetan* | *to do good, be of benefit* |
| *der Handy-Freak, -s* | *cell phone freak* |
| *der Handy-Hasser, –* | *cell phone hater* |
| *der Handy-Normalo, -s* | *person who deals with cell phones in a well-adjusted, "normal" manner* |
| *der Handytyp, -en* | *cell phone guy* |
| *kalt·lassen, es hat kaltgelassen* | *to leave cold* |
| *der Klingelton, ¨e* | *ring tone* |
| *die Kurznachricht, -en* | *short message* |
| *der Mitmensch, -en* | *fellow human being* |
| *nerven* | *to annoy* |
| nirgends | nowhere |
| pausenlos | non-stop, incessant |
| plötzlich | suddenly |
| das Portemonnaie, -s | wallet |
| *romantisch* | *romantic* |
| *ständig* | *constantly* |
| *teilweise* | *partially* |
| tolerant | tolerant |
| unangenehm | unpleasant |

### Seite 34 — page 34

| | |
|---|---|
| auf·fordern | to instruct, command |
| *befragen* | *to survey, poll* |
| *die Befragung, -en* | *survey, poll* |
| die Beziehung, -en | relationship |
| Bitteschön. | here: Here you are/here you go. |

| deutlich | clearly |
|---|---|
| doppelt | double |
| *die Ernährung (Sg)* | *nutrition* |
| *die Faust, ⸚e* | *fist* |
| *die Flatrate, -s* | *flat rate for service (i.e. cell phone)* |
| *die Frauensprache (Sg)* | *women's language* |
| gebrauchen | to use |
| *heraus·finden, er hat herausgefunden* | *to find out* |
| *indirekt* | *indirect* |
| die Konferenz, -en | conference |
| *die Konfliktsituation, -en* | *conflict situation* |
| *kooperativ* | *cooperative* |
| der Liebling, -e | darling |
| das Lieblingsthema, -themen | favorite topic |
| *die Männersprache (Sg)* | *men's language* |
| das Missverständnis, -se | misunderstanding |
| *mit Hilfe* | *with the aid (of)* |
| *das Nichtzutreffende (Sg)* | *the non-applicable (one)* |
| sondern | rather |
| *die Theorie, -n* | *theory* |
| unterbrechen, du unterbrichst, er unterbricht, er hat unterbrochen | to interrupt |
| das Vorurteil, -e | prejudice |

## Seite 35 — page 35

| *der bestimmte Artikel, –* | *definite article* |
|---|---|
| der Zweifel, – | doubt |

## Seite 36 — page 36

| *unappetitlich* | *unappetizing* |
|---|---|
| *unaufgeräumt* | *not straightened up* |
| *unentschieden* | *undecided* |
| ungemütlich | not cozy |
| unsauber | unclean |
| unselbstständig | not independent |
| *unverstanden* | *not understood* |

## Seite 37 — page 37

| *raus·fliegen, er ist rausgeflogen* | *to fly out* |
|---|---|
| der Schwiegersohn, ⸚e | son-in-law |
| *unerzogen* | *ill-bred, uneducated* |
| ungern | not gladly or happily |
| uninteressant | uninteresting |
| unmodern | not modern, non-modern |
| *unnötig* | *unnecessary* |
| *unpassend* | *not fitting, non-fitting* |
| unpünktlich | not punctual, non-punctual |
| unvorsichtig | not careful, careless |

## Arbeitsbuch — Workbook

### Seite 103 — page 103

| *der Päckchenschein, -e* | *package label* |
|---|---|
| *das Sprichwort, ⸚er* | *saying* |

### Seite 105 — page 105

| *aus·schneiden, er hat ausgeschnitten* | *to cut out* |
|---|---|
| das Hochzeitsfest, -e | wedding celebration |

### Seite 106 — page 106

| *die Digitalkamera, -s* | *digital camera* |
|---|---|
| *der Flachbildschirm, -e* | *flatscreen* |
| der Fußballschuh, -e | football shoe |
| *der Kunstreiseführer, –* | *art guidebook for tourists* |

### Seite 107 — page 107

| fressen, er frisst, er hat gefressen | to eat (used for animals) |
|---|---|
| das Treffen, – | meeting, encounter |

### Seite 108 — page 108

| erreichen | here: to catch, make, board on time |
|---|---|
| fehlerlos | error-free |
| fleischlos | meatless |
| kinderlos | childless |
| *phantasielos* | *devoid of imagination* |
| planlos | without a plan |
| ruhelos | agitated, lacking calmness |
| *die Wortfamilie, -n* | *word family* |

### Seite 109 — page 109

| *die Besorgung, -en* | *errand, procurement* |
|---|---|
| *der Direktor, -en* | *director* |
| *die Entscheidung, -en* | *decision* |
| *die Erwartung, -en* | *expectation* |

### Seite 110 — page 110

| *die Telekommunikation, -en* | *telecommunications* |
|---|---|

## 1 Passive voice: present *(Passiv: Präsens)*

examples    *Hier **wird** die Adresse **reingeschrieben**.*
*(= Hier schreibt man die Adresse rein.)*

The address is written in here. (= This is where you write in the address.)

*Für die Päckchen **werden** diese Formulare **benutzt**.*
*(= Für die Päckchen benutzt man diese Formulare.)*

These forms are used for packages.
(= For packages, you use these forms.)

When describing a process or giving instructions in German, very often an impersonal construction using the indefinite pronoun *man* (like the English "one" or the impersonal "you" in speech) is used, or the passive voice of the verb can be used. As opposed to the active voice, where the verb's subject acts ("the label uses"), the passive voice allows the verb's subject to be acted upon ("the label is used"). German uses the passive voice more than English does, though it primarily occurs in writing.

The passive voice in German is constructed using the verb *werden* as the conjugated, auxiliary verb, and the past participle of the verb in question:

|  |  | form of *werden* | participle |
|---|---|---|---|
| singular | *Die Adresse* | ***wird** hier* | ***reingeschrieben**.* |
| plural | *Diese Formulare* | ***werden** für Päckchen* | ***benutzt**.* |

## 2 Adjective declension: definite article *(Adjektivdeklination: bestimmter Atikel)*

| examples |  | nominative |  |
|---|---|---|---|
| **m** | *Der **alte** Computer funktioniert gut.* | | The old computer works well. |
| **n** | *Das **rote** Handy gefällt mir.* | | I like the red cell phone. |
| **f** | *Die **digitale** Kamera hier ist toll.* | | The digital camera here is great. |
| **pl** | *Die **neuen** Kataloge sind da.* | | The new catalogues are in. |

In Chapter 9, we learned the endings for adjectives that precede nouns with indefinite articles: *ein schöner Ring, ein originelles Foto, eine billige Lampe, alte Uhren* (m, n, f, pl).

As we also saw, nouns with definite articles *(der, die, das)* take only the endings *-e* and *-en* in the nominative, since the article indicates the gender, case and number. The definite articles in the other cases also serve this function, and thus there are only two possible endings:

|  | nominative | accusative | dative |  |
|---|---|---|---|---|
| **m** | *der schöne* | *den schönen* | *dem schönen* | *Ring* |
| **n** | *das originelle* | *das originelle* | *dem originellen* | *Foto* |
| **f** | *die billige* | *die billige* | *der billigen* | *Lampe* |
| **pl** | *die alten* | *die alten* | *den alten* | *Uhren* |

## 3 Interrogative construction *Was für ein ...?* (*Fragepartikel „Was für ein?"*)

### a nominative

examples

| *Was für ein Mensch ist er?* | What kind of a person is he? |
| *Was für eine Lampe ist das?* | What kind of a lamp ist that? |
| *Was für Kurse sind das?* | What kind of classes are those? |

With the interrogative construction *Was für ein...?* the speaker can solicit information about the type, class or other qualifier relating to someone or something. The *ein* within the construction agrees with the noun in question. Note that when asking about a plural noun, *ein* has no plural form, so the construction becomes *was für*.

### b accusative

examples

| *Was für einen Beruf hat er?* | What kind of a profession does he have? |
| *Was für Hobbys hat er?* | What kinds of hobbies does he have? |

Since the *ein* in the construction agrees with the noun, it also reflects the noun's case.
In the accusative, that will involve the change from *ein* to *einen*: *Was für einen Beruf hat er?*
(→ *haben* + accusative).

Remember: when asking about an individual person or thing within a group, the interrogative *welch-?* is used (in English, "which?" versus "what kind of?"). To review this, see *Schritte international 2*, Chapter 13.

*Welches Kleid soll ich anziehen, das blaue oder das schwarze?*
*Welchen Schauspieler magst du am liebsten?*

## 4 Word formation *(Wortbildung)*

### a adjective/adverb (positive) → adjective/adverb (negative)

examples

| *Diesen Klingelton finde ich **angenehm**,* | I think this ring tone is pleasant, |
| *aber diesen hier finde ich sehr **unangenehm**.* | but this one I think is unpleasant. |

German uses the prefix *un-* just as English uses both *un-* and *in-/im-* to convert adjectives from a positive to a negative or opposite. But take note! Not all modifiers use a prefix to form their opposites. Below is a list of some of the most common adjectives/adverbs that use *un-*. As you review your vocabulary from prior lessons, and moving into future units, you will want to add to the list.

| *bequem* (comfortable) | → *unbequem* (uncomfortable) |
| *flexibel* (flexible) | → *unflexibel* (inflexible) |
| *freundlich* (friendly) | → *unfreundlich* (unfriendly) |
| *gemütlich* (inviting) | → *ungemütlich* (uninviting) |
| *glücklich* (happy) | → *unglücklich* (unhappy) |
| *höflich* (polite) | → *unhöflich* (impolite) |
| *interessant* (interesting) | → *uninteressant* (uninteresting) |
| *modern* (modern) | → *unmodern* (not modern) |
| *möglich* (possible) | → *unmöglich* (impossible) |
| *ordentlich* (orderly) | → *unordentlich* (disorderly) |

| | |
|---|---|
| *professionell* (professional) | → *unprofessionell* (unprofessional) |
| *pünktlich* (punctual) | → *unpünktlich* (not punctual) |
| *ruhig* (calm) | → *unruhig* (restless, not calm, disquieted) |
| *sicher* (sure, certain) | → *unsicher* (unsure, uncertain) |
| *vorsichtig* (careful) | → *unvorsichtig* (careless) |
| *wichtig* (important) | → *unwichtig* (unimportant) |
| *zufrieden* (satisfied) | → *unzufrieden* (dissatisfied) |
| … | |

With modifiers using *un-*, the stress generally falls on the prefix with one notable exception: *unmöglich*.

**b**  noun → adjective

examples  *Anna kann stundenlang reden, **ohne Pause**.*  Anna can talk for hours, without a break.
*– Und Kevin sieht **pausenlos** fern.*  – And Kevin watches TV incessantly.

The suffix *-los* is equivalent to the preposition *ohne* (without) and functions much like the English *-less*. Ascertaining the meaning of an adjective or adverb ending in *-los*, it helps to understand the meaning of the noun upon which it is built. Following is a representative selection of modifiers using *-los*:

| | |
|---|---|
| *ohne Arbeit* | → *arbeitslos* (unemployed) |
| *ohne Ende* | → *endlos* (endless) |
| *ohne Grund* | → *grundlos* (without reason, baseless) |
| *ohne Hilfe* | → *hilflos* (helpless) |
| *ohne Kinder* | → *kinderlos* (childless) |
| *ohne Kosten* | → *kostenlos* (free of charge) |
| *ohne Lust* | → *lustlos* (listless, half-hearted) |
| *ohne Probleme* | → *problemlos* (problem-free) |
| *ohne Schlaf* | → *schlaflos* (sleepless) |
| *ohne Sinn* | → *sinnlos* (senseless) |
| … | |

**c**  verb → noun

examples  *Sollten wir das nicht **üben**?*  Shouldn't we practice this?
*– Ja, machen Sie bitte die **Übung** 3.*  – Yes, do exercise 3, please.

Many verbs (but not all!) can be converted to nouns by using the suffix *-ung*.
When you encounter a new noun ending in *-ung*, consider the meaning of the verb it is built upon in order to ascertain the noun's meaning.

| | |
|---|---|
| *befragen* | → *die Befragung* (survey, poll) |
| *einleiten* | → *die Einleitung* (introcution) |
| *erfahren* | → *die Erfahrung* (experience) |
| *ergänzen* | → *die Ergänzung* (completion) |
| *meinen* | → *die Meinung* (opinion) |
| *untersuchen* | → *die Untersuchung* (examination) |
| *wohnen* | → *die Wohnung* (apartment) |

Any noun ending in *-ung* is, of course, feminine.

**5**    **Translate into English.**

**a**   *Hier wird ein großer Supermarkt gebaut.*

........................................................

*– Ach ja? In dieser Straße gibt es doch schon*

........................................................

*zwei.*

........................................................

**b**   *Was ist mit der neuen Kamera?*

........................................................

*– Sie wird gerade getestet. Wenn alles in*

........................................................

*Ordnung ist, wird sie nächsten Monat auf*

........................................................

*den Markt gebracht.*

........................................................

**c**   *Über das Thema „Frauensprache –*

........................................................

*Männersprache" wird in letzter Zeit viel*

........................................................

*diskutiert.*

........................................................

*– Stimmt, und was ist deine Meinung?*

........................................................

**d**   *Die Fenster in unserem Büro sind schon*

........................................................

*ganz schmutzig.*

........................................................

*– Werden die denn nie geputzt?*

........................................................

**6**    **Translate into English.**

**a**   *Ich suche ein schönes Buch für meinen*

........................................................

*Kollegen.*

........................................................

*– Was für Bücher liest er denn gern?*

........................................................

**b**   *Ich würde mir gern ein neues Fahrrad*

........................................................

*kaufen.*

........................................................

*– Was für ein Fahrrad möchtest du denn?*

........................................................

*Ein Mountainbike.*

........................................................

**c**   *Wenn Sie zwei DVDs kaufen, bekommen Sie*

........................................................

*die dritte kostenlos.*

........................................................

*– Prima, dann nehme ich vier.*

........................................................

**d**   *Die alte Kuckucksuhr geht ganz ungenau.*

........................................................

*Wir müssen sie mal zur Reparatur bringen.*

........................................................

*– Ich kann sie morgen mitnehmen.*

........................................................

**7**    **Translate into German.**

**a**    How do you make apple strudel?    .................................... *man* ....................

– I don't know. We could look for the    ................................................................

recipe on the internet.    ................................................................

**b**    They work a lot here, but they earn a lot,    *Hier wird* ........................................

too. Does the job interest you?    ........................................ *die Stelle?*

– I'm not sure.    ................................................................

**c**    How do you like the new (picture) screen?    ................................................................

– Very much, much better than the old one.    ................................................................

**d**    I think I'll buy the red pullover with the    ................................................................

white stripes.    ................................................................

– I wouldn't buy that one. I like the yellow    ................................................................

one better.    ................................................................

**8**    **Translate into German.**

**a**    What kinds of questions appear on the test?    .................... *kommen* ....................

– None about grammar.    ................................................................

**b**    Which cell phone do you like better, the    ................................................................

black one or the blue one?    ................................................................

– The blue one. Do you want a case for it,    ................................................................

too?    ................................................................

**c**    I'm never going into this store again. The    ................................................................

saleswoman is very disagreeable.    ................................................................

– Yeah, she's impolite and does her work    ................................................................

lethargically.    ................................................................

**d**    What sort of plans do you all have for the    ................................................................

weekend?    ................................................................

– I don't know yet. Perhaps we'll drive    ................................................................

into the mountains.    ................................................................

## Listening and Pronunciation

### b – d – g  /  p – t – k (or ch)

In spoken German, the consonants [b], [d] and [g] will often sound different at the end of a syllable than at the beginning.

### [b]

In the initial position, [b] is pronounced identically to the English letter:
*Bäcker, Brot*

But at the end of a word, as what the Germans call an *Auslaut*, the voiced [b] becomes voiceless and resembles [p]. Hence, the English name "Bob" often sounds more like "bop" when spoken by a German. There are relatively few words in German that end with [b]:
*ab, Schub, Hieb,* and whenever a verb ending is dropped, such as *ich hab'*.

But usually, the [b] is followed by an [e], retaining the voiced quality of the [b]:
*Bube*

### [d]

Likewise, an initial [d] is identical to the English:
*Datum, Dose*

But again, it loses its voicing at the end of a word and becomes more akin to a [t]:
*Leid, Hand, Pfund*

### [g]

The letter [g] in final position poses a bit more difficulty as it can have two different sounds, and when combined with an [n], yet one more.

When combined with *-i-* to form *-ig*, the [g] sounds more like [ch], forming the *ich-Laut* discussed in *Schritte international XXL-Glossar* Vol. 3, Chapter 6.
When it combines with an *-e-*, as in *Weg* or *weg*, the [g] loses its voice to sound more like [k]. This also happens with *-a-*, as in *Tag*.
And don't forget the [ng] cluster, which sounds just like the English version in, for example, *sing* (see *Schritte international* Glossary XXL Vol. 2, Chapter 12).

## Familiarity and Understanding

### Women's suffrage
*„Endlich, endlich, endlich ... – ... allgemeines, gleiches, direktes und geheimes Stimmrecht für alle Staatsbürger ohne Unterschied des Geschlechts"*

Though numerous regions in Europe had done so prior (Corsica in 1755, the Isle of Man in 1881), the majority of central European states allowed women the right to vote after World War I, with the Scandanavian states leading the way (Finland was first in 1906).

Of the three German-speaking countries, Austria became the first to grant women the vote on November 12, 1918, coinciding with the abolition of the Austro-Hungarian monarchy and the adoption of the Austro-German Republic Constitution.

German women won the vote at almost the same time, again owing to the adoption of a new constitution. In the election of January 19, 1919, women were allowed to vote for and run for seats in the National Assembly. As a result, 40 of the 400 deputies were women.

As was the case with suffrage for women in the United States, the arguments used against women voting now appear to be ludicrous. Chief among them: women who did not serve in the military could not possess a sense of national responsibility necessary to vote; and women could not read serious articles in newspapers and thus could not understand the issues involved in elections. Still, both Austria and Germany granted universal suffrage ahead of the United States, which did not amend its Constitution to allow women to vote until 1920.

Switzerland's Confederation, which gives far more power to the cantons than to the central government, has the most curious suffrage history of all. The democratic process in Switzerland has deep roots, and giving women the right to vote required passage of a referendum. The first referendum on women's suffrage was brought to a vote in 1957, but with only men voting (save for the canton of Valais, where 33 of 84 women cast votes in favor of suffrage before their votes were declared illegal) the measure was defeated. Not until 1973 did Swiss women receive the right to vote in federal elections. Cantonal elections, however, were another matter. The final canton to grant suffrage to women was Appenzell-Innerrhoden, shortly after the fall of the Berlin Wall in 1990. Liechtenstein, the tiny duchy between Austria and Switzerland, did not allow female citizens to actively express their opinions at the ballot box until 1984.

### That random *"I"*

Readers of German texts often come across what appears to be a feminine form with a typo: *LehrerInnen, StudentInnen*, etc.
This capital "i" within these words began to appear in the 1980s to denote that both male and female professionals were being addressed or described, in the case of *LehrerInnen*.
This spelling has never been officially accepted, as capital letters may only appear at the beginning of a word. Still, it continues to be used frequently. Other ways of expressing mixed-gender groups are: *Lehrer(innen)* or *Lehrerinnen und Lehrer.*

### Leibniz

Speaking on cell phones, listening to music on CDs or writing e-mail: all these technologies we take for granted, indeed, all computer-based technologies are based upon binary code.

Binary code takes its name from the fact that it is based on two numerals, 0 and 1. The first person to systematically document this concept, comparing 1 with the spirit of God and 0 with nothing, predicting that the combination of these two digits would lead to "amazing advantages", lived in the 17th century.

Gottfried Wilhelm Leibniz (Leipzig 1646 – Hannover 1716) was a mathematician, philosopher, scientist, diplomat and a scholar of history, law and theology, enjoying success in all these fields not only in Germany but also in France and England. He was a member of the Royal Academies of Science in London (where he met Newton) and Berlin, and served as the privy councillor to numerous rulers throughout his lifetime.

His greatest successes came in philosophy and in mathematics. He invented an infinitesimal calculus which Newton claimed Leibniz stole from him; Newton's claim was upheld at the time but research since has proven that Leibniz's calculus differs significantly from Newton's, and in light of 20th century advances in relativity, is in some regards even more refined.

Prefiguring the computers that would owe their existence to his binary system, Leibniz also invented a calculator that could perform the four basic arithmetic functions.

Leibniz' infatiguability is evinced in the over 15,000 letters that he wrote to over 1,000 correspondents alongside his published writings during his own lifetime, and the volumes that remained unpublished after his death. To this day, there is no single complete edition of all of his work.

For many years, Leibniz's reputation suffered first under the weight of Newton's accusations, and then under Voltaire's attack on his theodicy, which his student Christian Wolff carried to extremes after Leibniz's death. Voltaire's novel *Candide* was actually an attack on Wolff's misinterpretation of Leibniz's philosophy, but the stain remained for generations. In recent years, however, he has again been acknowledged as one of the last universal scholars and scientists and the first truly modern thinker.

## Historical Fragments

### Merchants, pirates, and wars: The Hanseatic League

From 1260 until approximately 1669, there existed *die Deutsche Hanse*, The German Hansa, also known as the Hanseatic League, an association first of merchants and then of entire cities. First organized to fight pirates such as Klaus Störtebeker and the *Likedeeler* (see *Schritte international XXL Glossary* Vol. 2, Chapter 12), the League existed first and foremost to protect and to cultivate the commercial interests of its members. From the 13th century on, the Hansa owned the Baltic Sea and controlled all trade along its shores.

At its zenith, almost 200 cities were members of the Hansa. Their common interest was safety and security of trade routes, particularly those by sea, where a new type of shipping vessel, the *Kogge*, was emerging. A *Kogge* could transport loads of 120 to 200 tons (almost 100 times the load that one automobile can carry) moving at an average speed of 4 to 6 mph. (One mile in this period equalled 1,853 meters, longer than the 1670 meters of the modern mile.) A trip from Lübeck to Bergen, Norway, took no more than 3 to 4 weeks, while Riga to the coast of France lasted 2 to 3 months.

Member cities and merchants traded furs, beeswax, honey, salt (particularly from Lüneburg), beer (especially from Hamburg), Swedish iron, copper, butter and lard, Scandanavian cod and herring, hemp and grains, but they also carried silk, oil, wool and cloth from Flanders.
The bulk of transport was by sea. The most important route created a line from Novgorod to Reval (Riga, now Latvia) then to Lübeck, onto Hamburg and London, crossing the Baltic Sea and the North Sea. Lübeck became the Hansa's capital and the most important trading point between the Baltic and western Europe. In many port cities, merchants enjoyed special privileges, demonstrated by their separate neighborhoods. In London (Steelyard, *Stalhof*), in Bergen, Norway (*Die deutsche Brücke* – "the German bridge"), in Novgorod (*Peterhof* – "St. Peter's Courtyard", also known as *Torgovyi Ryad* today) and in Bruges, Belgium, there existed *Kontore* (counting-houses), where princes and government officials effectively never entered, as the Hansa held jurisdiction.

The Hansa's language was *Plattdeutsch* (low German) with all trade negotiated in that tongue, all contracts and regulations recorded in it. To this day, traces of German influence as a result of this interaction can be found in all Baltic languages as well as in Russian. The political, economic and cultural influence of the Hansa grew so great that it once declared war on the state of Denmark. The Treaty of Stralsund was signed in 1370, giving the League a share of Danish trade profits and allowing for the Danish King's election without the Hansa's consent.

Years later, the Hansa lost to Denmark when the latter gained control over transit between the North and Baltic Seas, and boats were required to pay fees to pass across the straits under Denmark's control. Further decline ensued upon the colonization of North America, reducing the overall importance of Baltic trade. The continued rise of individual nations' power further eroded the Hansa's monopoly on commerce. England, Portugal, the Netherlands and France increased their maritime presence and strength, and expanded their commercial domains. In Russia, Tsar Ivan III destroyed the *Peterhof* in 1478 to drive foreign merchants out of Novgorod; and a century later, England's Queen Elizabeth I closed the Steelyard (*Stalhof*) and expelled the League.

During the Thirty Years War, the Hansa lost its remaining strength as the populations of its member cities were decimated and commercial trade came to a virtual standstill. Many of the member cities lay in ruins, with one notable exception: Hamburg proved to be inconquearable and thus retained its independence.
Nevertheless, until the 19th century, there was no German maritime fleet to speak of. Only when Prussia emerged as the dominant power in Germany and launched into war against Denmark did the beginnings of a German navy appear.

Today, the memory of the Hansa is still present in some northern German cities, particularly in Hamburg, Bremen, Lübeck, Rostock, Stralsund and Greifswald. There are signs elsewhere in Europe; the League has taken on a modern role of fostering better business links, tourism and cultural exchange, helping to restore, for example the *Torgovyi Ryad (Peterhof)* in Novgorod, Russia as part of the historic old city there.

## Self-Evaluation

**Communication**

### When listening, I can understand (Hören)

– short advertisements on specific products: *die verrückten Handytaschen von Diana*
– phone messages left on an answering machine: *„Hier Praxis Dr. Camerer. Wir müssen leider den Termin für Ihre Untersuchung und Grippeimpfung verschieben."*
– an interview with diverse individuals on a particular topic: *„Heute hat fast jeder Jugendliche ein Handy! Wie finden Sie das?"*

### In written texts, I can understand (Lesen)

– tests and the summary of the results: *„Welcher Handytyp sind Sie?"*
– survey results: *„Er spricht am liebsten über seinen Beruf, über Musik, Nachrichten und Sport."*
– letters, e-mails and simple cards: *„Lieber Lukas, schön, dass du mich bald besuchst."*
– a simple song lyric: *„Ich fühle mich so unverstanden ..."*

### I can produce the following oral structures (Sprechen)

– excusing myself: *„Es tut mir schrecklich leid, dass ich gestern nicht gekommen bin."*
– recounting a story: *„Aber dann stellt Maria fest, dass ..."*
– interpreting test results: *„Also, der Test sagt, ich bin der Handy-Freak. Das stimmt. Ich telefoniere wirklich sehr gerne mit dem Handy."*
– state my opinion based on my own experiences: *„Frauen reden mehr als Männer."*

### I can produce the following written texts (Schreiben)

– invitations and suggestions: *„Liebe ..., komm doch mal nach Frankfurt. Ich möchte dir so gern den ‚Römer' zeigen."*
– an e-mail: *„Liebe Claudia, gerade habe ich ..."*

| Kursbuch | Textbook |
|---|---|
| **Seite 38** | **page 38** |
| die Batterie, -n | battery |
| das Benzin (Sg) | gasoline, petrol |
| der Diesel (Sg) | diesel |
| das Kennzeichen, – | license plate |
| das KFZ, – | passenger vehicle |
| der KFZ-Schein, -e | passenger vehicle certificate |
| der Motor, -en | motor |
| tanken | to put gas in the tank |
| der Wagen, – | car, automobile |
| die Werkstatt, ⁻en | repair shop |

| **Seite 39** | **page 39** |
|---|---|
| fest·stellen | to ascertain |
| für etwas sein | to be in favor of something |
| *der Schokoriegel, –* | *candy bar, chocolate bar* |

| **Seite 40** | **page 40** |
|---|---|
| die Garage, -n | garage |
| *die Pantomime, -n* | *pantomime* |
| *pantomimisch* | *pantomimic* |
| *umgekehrt* | *vice versa* |
| *der Zahnarzt, ⁻e* | *dentist* |

| **Seite 41** | **page 41** |
|---|---|
| ab·biegen, er ist abgebogen | to turn into a street |
| das Bahngleis, -e | rail track |
| die Brücke, -n | bridge |
| entlang·fahren, du fährst entlang, er fährt entlang, er ist entlanggefahren | to drive along (something) |
| entlang·gehen, er ist entlanggegangen | to go along (something) |
| das Flussufer, – | riverbank |
| die Haltestelle, -n | bus stop |
| *der Kreisverkehr, -e* | *traffic circle, roundabout* |
| *der Kursort, -e* | *location of class* |
| die Sprachenschule, -n | language school |
| um … herum | around |
| weiter·fahren, du fährst weiter, er fährt weiter, er ist weitergefahren | to drive farther, continue driving |

| **Seite 42** | **page 42** |
|---|---|
| die Bremse, -n | brake |
| bremsen | to brake |
| *der Bremsweg, -e* | *braking distance* |
| dabei haben | to have at one's disposal |
| *einwandfrei* | *faultlessly, flawlessly* |
| erkennbar | recognizable |
| erreichbar | achievable |
| Fall: auf jeden Fall | case; in any case |
| der Fußgänger, – | pedestrian |
| glatt | slick |
| *der Helm, -e* | *helmet* |
| *die Klingel, -n* | *bell* |
| nass | wet |
| die Panne, -n | flat tire |
| der Radfahrer, – | cyclist |
| der Reifen, – | tire |
| das Rücklicht, -er | light in back |
| *der Sicherheits-Check, -s* | *safety check* |
| überholen | to pass (in traffic) |
| *das Vorderlicht, -er* | *light in front* |
| wechseln | to change |
| das Werkzeug (Sg) | tool |
| zurecht·kommen, er ist zurechtgekommen | to get by, make do |

| **Seite 43** | **page 43** |
|---|---|
| die Autobahn, -en | high-speed highway |
| die Aussicht, -en | view |
| *aus·weichen, er ist ausgewichen* | *to avoid* |
| *blockieren* | *to block* |
| *böig* | *gusty* |
| der Bürgermeister, – | mayor |
| dicht | dense |
| *ein·weihen* | *to dedicate* |
| *eisig* | *icy* |
| *die Endstation, -en* | *end of the line, final station* |
| *der Flieger, –* | *here: planes* |
| gewittrig | stormy |
| komplett | completely |
| kräftig | powerful |
| kühl | cool (temperature) |
| *lahm·legen* | *to paralyze* |
| landen | to land |
| die Landung, -en | landing |
| der Nebel, – | fog |
| neblig | foggy |
| der Nordwesten (Sg) | Northwest |
| *der Regenschauer, –* | *rain shower* |
| regnerisch | rainy |
| die Richtung, -en | direction |
| der Schnee (Sg) | snow |
| *sperren* | *to block, close* |

| | |
|---|---|
| der Start, -s | take-off |
| der Stau, -s | traffic jam |
| *strahlend* | *beaming* |
| der Sturm, ⸚e | storm |
| *stürmisch* | *stormy* |
| *vergangene* | *past (previous)* |
| *verhindern* | *to hinder* |
| der Verkehr (Sg) | traffic |
| die Verkehrsnachricht, -en | traffic news |
| weder … noch | neither … nor |
| *wehen: es weht* | *to blow (as in wind)* |
| die Wolke, -n | cloud |
| *wolkig* | *cloudy* |
| zum Teil | in part, to an extent |

## Seite 44 — page 44

| | |
|---|---|
| *abgebildet sein* | *to be pictured* |
| die Einbahnstraße, -n | one-way street |
| *ein·parken* | *to park* |
| die Fußgängerzone, -n | pedestrian zone |
| *der Gehweg, -e* | *walkway* |
| halten (sich … an), du hältst dich, er hält sich, er hat sich gehalten | to keep to |
| km/h | kilometers per hour |
| *der Radler, –* | *cyclist* |
| rücksichtslos | inconsiderate, reckless |
| die Verkehrsregel, -n | traffic regulation |
| der Verkehrsteilnehmer, – | participant in traffic |

## Seite 45 — page 45

| | |
|---|---|
| entlang | along |
| das Ufer, – | bank, shore |

## Seite 46 — page 46

| | |
|---|---|
| *der Abstand (Sg)* | *distance (between objects)* |
| das Blut (Sg) | blood |
| *die Fahrbahn, -en* | *traffic lane* |
| *fantastisch* | *fantastic* |
| *Gas geben* | *to step on the gas, accelerate* |
| mittlere | middle |
| *nördlichste* | *northernmost* |
| die Ortschaft, -en | *locality* |
| *das Promille, –* | *per thousand (measurement of blood alcohol content)* |
| *ran·fahren, du fährst ran, er fährt ran, er ist rangefahren* | *to drive up to something* |

| | |
|---|---|
| raus·fahren, du fährst raus, er fährt raus, er ist rausgefahren | to drive out, exit |
| die Spur, -en | here: lane |
| *der Tachowert, -e* | *value shown on the tachometer* |
| *das Traumland, ⸚er* | *dream country* |
| vorbei·lassen, du lässt vorbei, er lässt vorbei, er hat vorbeigelassen | to let pass |
| *der Vordermann, ⸚er* | *driver in front* |

## Seite 47 — page 47

| | |
|---|---|
| der Ausländer, – | foreigner |
| *der Bußgeldkatalog, -e* | *penalty index* |
| *dänisch* | *Danish* |
| *die Europäische Zentralbank (Sg)* | *European Central Bank* |
| *die Hafenstadt, ⸚e* | *port city* |
| *der Idiotentest, -s* | *idiot test* |
| *medizinisch-psychologisch* | *medical-psychological* |
| die Minderheit, -en | minority |
| *der Seehafen, ⸚* | *sea port* |
| um·drehen | to turn around |
| *das Verkehrszentralregister, –* | *registry of the central traffic office* |

## Arbeitsbuch — Workbook

## Seite 112 — page 112

| | |
|---|---|
| springen, er ist gesprungen | to jump |

## Seite 113 — page 113

| | |
|---|---|
| *das Bussi, -s* | *smooch, kiss* |
| der Fußballplatz, ⸚e | football/soccer field |

## Seite 114 — page 114

| | |
|---|---|
| *die Altstadt, ⸚e* | *old part of the city* |
| *das Altstadtparkhaus, ⸚er* | *parking garage in the old part of the city* |

## Seite 115 — page 115

| | |
|---|---|
| *die Cafeteria, -s/Cafeterien* | *cafeteria* |

| | |
|---|---|
| *das Sekretariat, -e* | *secretariat, office, registry* |
| der Stadtpark, -s | city park |

## Seite 116 — page 116

| | |
|---|---|
| *im Dunkeln* | *in the dark* |

## Seite 117 — page 117

| | |
|---|---|
| die Fahrradkleidung (Sg) | biking clothes |
| *das Quadrat, -e* | *square* |

## Seite 118 — page 118

| | |
|---|---|
| *ab·wechseln (sich)* | *to alternate, take turns* |
| jedoch | however, though, but |
| *der Schauer, –* | *(rain)shower* |
| sinken, er ist gesunken | to sink (intransitive) |
| *sommerlich* | *summery* |
| *das Tiefland (Sg)* | *lowland* |
| die Vorhersage, -n | forecast |
| der Westwind, -e | west wind |
| *das Wetterwort, ̈er* | *weather word* |

## Seite 119 — page 119

| | |
|---|---|
| beste Grüße | best regards |
| *die Sachen (Pl)* | *here: clothes* |
| der Wintermantel, ̈ | winter coat |

## Seite 120 — page 120

| | |
|---|---|
| *die Gräfin, -nen* | *countess* |
| das Kinderlied, -er | children's song |
| der Lastwagen, – | truck, lorry |
| senkrecht | vertical |

## Seite 121 — page 121

| | |
|---|---|
| das Gebäude, – | building |
| der Krankenwagen, – | ambulance |
| *der Marktplatz, ̈e* | *marketplace, market square* |
| *das Stadtmuseum, -museen* | *City Museaum* |
| waagerecht | horizontal |

# Forms and Structures

## 11

**1**   **Locational prepositions in response to the question: *woher*?**
**(*Lokale Präpositionen auf die Frage „Woher?"*)**

examples   *Woher kommst du denn jetzt?*        Where are you coming from now?
*Es ist ja schon drei Uhr!*          It's already three o'clock!
*– Ich komme **aus der Schule**, wir*   – I'm coming from school. We
*hatten heute eine Stunde länger.*     had an extra hour today.

***Woher** haben Sie denn die schönen Blumen?*   Where did you geth the beautiful flowers
*– Die sind **aus unserem Garten**.*           (from)? – They're from our garden.

Indication of a point of origin in response to the question *woher?* is given using the preposition *aus*.
You first saw this question form in *Schritte international 1*, Chapter 1:
*Woher kommen Sie? – Aus Spanien.*

In spoken German, the interrogative *woher?* can often split, with the last part coming at the end of the
phrase: *Wo kommst du denn jetzt her?*

*Aus* always requires the dative case, so the article of those place names which require one must also
reflect the dative, as in these examples:
*(der Iran)*            → *Farzad kommt aus dem Iran.*
*(das Baskenland)*      → *Dieser Tanz ist aus dem Baskenland.*
*(die Schweiz)*         → *Dieser Käse kommt aus der Schweiz.*
*(die USA)*             → *David und Lizzy kommen aus den USA.*

examples   *Holst du mal eine Flasche Wein **aus** dem Keller?*   Would you get a bottle of wine from the  basement?

*Kurt ist gerade **aus** dem Büro gegangen.*   Kurt just stepped out of the office.

*Meine Kinder sind erwachsen, sie sind*   My children are grown and are already
*schon **aus** dem Haus.*                 out of the house.

*Ich fahre schon mal das Auto **aus** der Garage.*   I'm already pulling the car out of the garage.

Note that *aus* not only works as "from" but also "out of" a particular space.

examples   *Woher kommt Anna denn jetzt? Es ist*   Where is Anna coming from now?
*ja schon drei Uhr morgens!*           It's three in the morning!
*– Sie kommt **von einer Party**.*      – She's coming from a party.

***Woher** hast du denn die schönen Blumen?*   Where did you get the lovely flowers (from)?
*– Die habe ich **von meinem Chef**.*           – I got them from my boss.

*Hey Marco, **woher** kommst du denn?*   Hey Marco, where are you coming from?
*– Ich komme **vom Training**.*          – I'm coming from practice.

Some questions with *woher?* elicit a response using *von*. *Von* indicates a point of departure, but not of
origin:
*Ich komme **aus** Sevilla  = I come from Seville (I was born there).
*Ich komme **von** Sevilla.* = I'm coming from Seville (I was just there before arriving here).
In contrast to *aus*, *von* is not associated with the interior of an enclosure, but rather more with an
activity that takes place there. *Von* is used with reference to:
– persons or institutions (*von meinem Chef, von der Polizei*),
– activities (*vom Training, von der Arbeit*) or
– celebrations (*von einer Party, von einer Hochzeit*).

examples  *Sie kommt gerade **vom** Supermarkt.*      She's coming from the supermarket.

*Sie kommt gerade **aus** dem Supermarkt.*  She's just coming out of the supermarket.

In the first sentence, the supermarket is the last place she was at before going to her next destination. The second sentence emphasizes her exit from the building.

In the examples with *von* note that, not only is the dative required, but the preposition *von* contracts with the masculine and neuter article *dem*: *von dem* → *vom*.

In review, here are some of the locational prepositions:

|  |  | origin:<br>*Woher?* | location:<br>*Wo?* | destination:<br>*Wohin?* |
|---|---|---|---|---|
| building,<br>enclosure | m<br>n<br>f<br>pl | *aus dem Garten*<br>*aus dem Auto*<br>*aus der Küche*<br>*aus den Zimmern* | *im Garten*<br>*im Auto*<br>*in der Küche*<br>*in den Zimmern* | *in den Garten*<br>*ins Auto*<br>*in die Küche*<br>*in die Zimmer* |
| businesses,<br>persons,<br>activities,<br>institutions | m<br>n<br>f<br>pl | *von Servitec*<br>*vom Metzger*<br>*vom Training*<br>*von der Polizei*<br>*von den Kollegen* | *bei Servitec*<br>*beim Metzger*<br>*beim Training*<br>*bei der Polizei*<br>*bei den Kollegen* | *zu Servitec*<br>*zum Metzger*<br>*zum Training*<br>*zur Polizei*<br>*zu den Kollegen* |
|  |  | *But note!*<br>*von zu Hause* | *zu Hause* | *nach Hause* |

## 2    Other locational prepositions *(Lokale Präpositionen)*

### a   with accusative

examples  *Müssen wir **durch** das Zentrum fahren?*      Do we have to drive through the center/downtown?
*Du musst **um** den Platz (herum) fahren.*      You have to go around the square/plaza.
*Ihr müsst hier die Straße **entlang** gehen.*      You have to go along the street here.
*Ihr fahrt jetzt **über** die Brücke da.*      You drive over the bridge there.

While the meanings of these prepositions are fairly straightforward, their location in sentences may seem a bit different at times, particularly in the case of the middle two:

| | |
|---|---|
| *durch* (through): | *durch den Wald, durch die Tür, durch die ganze Stadt* |
| *um ... herum* (around): | *um den Kopf herum, um den Kreisverkehr herum,*<br>*um die Insel herum* |
| *entlang* (along): | *den Fluss entlang, den Flur entlang, die Parkstraße entlang* |
| *über* (over, across): | *über die Kreuzung, über die Straße, über die Ampel* |

The first three prepositions here require the accusative. Note that *entlang* is actually a postposition, not a preposition, meaning that it comes **after** its object.
The preposition *über* requires accusative when indicating a destination, but requires dative when describing a location.

**b** with dative

examples

*Ihr müsst **bis zur** nächsten Ampel gehen.*
*Wir fahren **am** Bahnhof **vorbei.***
*Die Post liegt **gegenüber** der Schule.*

You have to go (up) to the next light.
We're driving past the train station.
The post office is accross from the school.

The prepositions *bis zu* and *an ... vobei* indicate movement in one direction, while *gegenüber* indicates a position. All require the dative case.

When heading destinations with proper names, *bis* does not combine with *zu*:
*Ich fahre bis Hamburg/bis Dänemark.*

When it describes a destination with an article, the *zu* is obligatory:
*Ich fahre bis zum Bahnhof / bis zur Haltestelle „Neumarkt" / bis zu den Kanarischen Inseln.*

*Gegenüber* used to be a postposition, but it is now heard as often as a preposition:
*Die Post liegt gegenüber der Schule. = Die Post liegt der Schule gegenüber.*

## 3  The conjunction *deshalb (Konjunktion „deshalb")*

examples

*Der Wagen ist schon alt.*
***Deshalb** müssen wir ihn dauernd*
*in die Werkstatt bringen.*

The car is already old.
Therefore/thus/for that reason
we constantly have to take it to
the shop.

*Elia möchte Ärztin werden.* ***Deshalb***
*studiert sie Medizin.*

Elia wants to become a doctor.
Therefore, she's studying medicine.

In its meaning of "thus" or "therefore", the conjunction *deshalb* is the opposite of *trotzdem* (see *Schritte international 4*, Chapter 8). But just like *trotzdem*, *deshalb* works differently than most conjunctions; its placement in a sentence is like that of an adverb. Instead of joining two sentences together to form one sentence, it usually begins the second, separate sentence instead. It can also follow the verb of the second clause. Both options are illustrated here below:

*Der Wagen ist schon alt. **Deshalb** müssen wir ihn dauernd in die Werkstatt bringen.*
*Der Wagen ist schon alt. Wir müssen ihn **deshalb** dauernd in die Werkstatt bringen.*

Remember the other conjunctions that indicate causality, and how those sentences are formed:

examples *Elia studiert Medizin, **weil** sie Ärztin werden möchte.* (verb in final position!)
*Elia studiert Medizin, **denn** sie möchte Ärztin werden.*

### 4 Word formation *(Wortbildung)*

#### a verb → adjective

examples | *Die Klingel ist gut **erreichbar**.* | The doorbell is easily reachable.
--- | --- | ---
| *= Man kann die Klingel gut erreichen.* | One can reach the doorbell easily.
| *Die Schilder sind gut **erkennbar**.* | The signs are easily recognizable.
| *= Man kann die Schilder gut erkennen.* |

The suffix *-bar* can often be added to the stem of a verb (such as *erreich-, erkenn-*) to convert it into an adjective. The suffix *-bar* signifies possiblity or abilty. From the examples above, you can see that very often, an adjective ending in *-bar* can be replaced with the construction *man kann + Infinitiv*; the use of an *-bar* adjective is a passive construction for the same.

In English, the suffixes "-ible/-able" fulfill the same function as the German *-bar* (which is also clear from the examples above) but you should be aware that not all "-ible/-able" adjectives in English have German *-bar* equivalents.

#### b noun → adjective

examples | *(Regen)* | *Heute ist es **regnerisch**.* | It's rainy today.
--- | --- | --- | ---
| *(Sturm)* | *Es weht ein **stürmischer** Wind.* | A stormy wind is blowing.
| *(Vorsicht)* | *Bitte fahren Sie **vorsichtig**!* | Please drive carefully!
| *(Wolken)* | *Am Morgen ist es **wolkig**.* | In the morning, it will be cloudy.

Adjectives ending in *-ig* or in *-isch* are generally derived from nouns. So if you run into a new adjective ending with either of these suffixes, stop and think if you already know the noun stem. You can then extrapolate the adjectival meaning. Keep in mind that very often, as you see in the examples above, both *-ig* and *-isch* correspond to the English -y suffix, but not always.

On some nouns, usually one-syllable, the vowel may umlaut when a suffix is added:

*Sturm – stürmisch*
*Kraft – kräftig*

For reasons of pronunciation, some nouns will also drop an unstressed *-e-* when taking the suffix *-ig* or *-isch*:

*Nebel → neblig*
*Gewitter → gewittrig*

### 5 Translate into English.

a | *Möchtet ihr frische Brötchen? Ich* | ...................................................................................
--- | --- | ---
| *komme gerade vom Einkaufen.* | ...................................................................................
| *– Nein danke, wir waren gerade beim* | ...................................................................................
| *Bäcker und haben selbst welche mitgebracht.* | ...................................................................................

**b** *Hallo Monika, hier ist Manfred. Ich* .................................................

*steige gerade aus dem Bus, in fünf* .................................................

*Minuten bin ich bei euch.* .................................................

**c** *Woher hast du denn diesen schicken Gürtel?* .................................................

*– Den habe ich von meiner Schwester* .................................................

*bekommen. Sie hat ihn in München* .................................................

*gekauft.* .................................................

**d** *Wir hatten eine Panne. Deshalb kommen* .................................................

*wir erst jetzt.* .................................................

*– Keine Sorge, Sie kommen trotzdem noch* .................................................

*früh genug. Wir haben noch nicht* .................................................

*angefangen.* .................................................

**6** **Translate into English.**

**a** *Entschuldigung, wie komme ich bitte* .................................................

*zum Bahnhof?* .................................................

*– Fahren Sie bis zur nächsten Kreuzung,* .................................................

*dort biegen Sie rechts ab und dann* .................................................

*an der Ampel wieder rechts.* .................................................

**b** *Bernd hat gesagt, wir müssen um den* .................................................

*Spielplatz herum und dann die Schiller-* .................................................

*straße entlang.* .................................................

*– Ja, aber ich glaube, wir sind falsch* .................................................

*gegangen. Wir sind jetzt in der Goethestraße.* ...........................

**c** *Kann man eigentlich mit dem Handy* .................................................

*auch scannen?* .................................................

*– Ja, das ist heute machbar.* .................................................

**d** *Wer hat denn das Päckchen angenommen?* .................................................

*– Ich weiß nicht. Die Unterschrift auf dem* .................................................

*Lieferschein ist nicht lesbar.* *delivery note* ............................

**7**  **Translate into German.**

**a**  I'll be done in a second. Can you get/
fetch the bikes from the basement?
– Yes, but hurry up.

...................................... *gleich* ......................................

......................................................................

......................................................................

**b**  Where were you? Your face is completely
red!
– I'm coming from playing football.

......................................................................

.......................................... *im Gesicht!*

......................................................................

**c**  How do you get to the library?
– Go through the park here, and then turn
left. Go along Park Street up to the light.
Then turn right.

......................................................................

......................................................................

......................................................................

......................................................................

**d**  One can get a flat (tire). For that reason,
one must have tools.

......................................................................

.................. *dabei* ......................................

**e**  Why do you need a dictionary?
– Because I don't understand this text.

......................................................................

......................................................................

**8**  **Translate into German.**

**a**  You can't drink this water. Didn't you
read the sign?
– Oh, it's not potable?

......................................................................

......................................................................

......................................................................

**b**  These mushrooms look very good. Can
you eat them?
– No, be careful, they're not edible!

.................... *Pilze* ......................................

......................................................................

......................................................................

**c**  How is the weather there in New York?
What sort of clothes should I bring?
– It's sunny, but bring an umbrella. It
might rain.

*Wie* ................ *bei euch in* ..............?

......................................................................

......................................................................

*Vielleicht* ..........................................

## Listening and Pronunciation

Pronunciation of the consonant clusters <pf>, <qu>, <ks> and <ts> are pronounced in German exactly as they are written.

### [pf]

Thus, the cluster [pf] requires putting the lips together to form the [p] before opening them and allowing air to pass and form the [f].

<pf> [pf] *Pfanne, Pflanze*

### [ts]

The combination [ts] is pronounced just as in the English word "hits" with both letters sounding. You will recall that this is also the sound of the German [z].
In the case of nouns ending with the suffix -*tion* (i.e., Nation), the -*t*- of the suffix has the same sound as [ts].

*Zentrum, Kreuzung, Rätsel*
*Lektion, Nation, Nationalität*

### [ks]

With respect to [ks], it is pronounced the same as <x>, which is the same in both German and English, like in the word 'Taxi'.

### [q]

<q> always appears with <u> (<qu>), and is pronounced [kv], like the Yiddish word kvetch, which originally comes from the German.

*bequem, Qualität*

## Familiarity and Understanding

### The continuing controversy of the *ess-zett*

Few events in recent German history have created as much uproar as the spelling reform. In 1996, the ministers of culture of the German-speaking countries created a commission to better standardize spelling across all three countries, facilitating learning and usage of German. The panel's recommendations in 1998 met with nearly universal disdain and rejection, especially in Germany, and were seen as unnecessary complications that had in fact been intended to simplify spelling, usage, plural forms, capitalization and so forth.

The best known of the new rules governed the use of "ß" which henceforth was to only be used after long vowels, while short vowels would be followed by "ss" – *Straße, du musst* – instead of the earlier *du mußt,* and *dass* (the conjunction) – which had previously been *daß.* Many critics insisted that this simplified nothing, citing numerous examples of cases where the distinction was still not clear, and newspapers, most notably the *Frankfurter Allgemeine Zeitung*, outrightly rejected the reform. Hundreds of writers at the Frankfurt Book Fair signed a petition protesting the reform.

Such widespread protest was completely unexpected, but clearly any changes to the common language, no matter how much people might complain otherwise, seemed to hit a very sensitive nerve. Academics were also troubled by some of the processes used to arrive at the commission's consensus, citing philological concerns.

After years of outrage and protest, there seemed to be a settling in 2004. After consultation with an independent board of review, the bulk of the initial reform was accepted, though some rules were adapted or amended to create a "third path". Schools now teach spelling according to the Orthographic Reform of August 1, 2005. None of this is retroactive, however, and materials published prior to 2005 are of course everywhere. There will exist an overlap, as there did with all prior reform measures. One of the funniest parodies of this irony occurred the year before the 2005 reform when *der Spiegel* and the Springer Verlag decided, after surveying their writers, to reject the spelling reform, prompting the satirical magazine *Titanic* to reject all 20th century spelling reforms and to publish the September 2004 issue cover according to rules set in the 19th century, including the old style *Fraktur* typeset. Eventually, most media outlets adopted their own in-house rules for orthography, based primarily on the 2005 reform but still cherry picking several matters according to taste.

All this was precisely what the "founder" of the first spelling reform had hoped to avoid: Konrad Duden (1829–1911) set forth the suggestion of standardization at a time when every publisher, ministry, university and poet did as they pleased when it came to writing German. In 1876, five years after the establishment of the German Empire, the first orthographic conference was convened. It should come as no surprise that after much tribulation, the first spelling reform failed: Konrad Duden championed a phonetically based approach, encouraging writing that followed speech, but opposition particularly from classically trained philologists was strong; they felt that words from Latin and Greek should reflect their roots and not contemporary German use (or corruption, depending upon one's perspective). Konrad Duden proceeded to write a compendium of basic rules of spelling and added a dictionary of 28,000 words written "properly".

The news was not all bad, however: Konrad Duden, whose name lives on in the dictionaries and language reference volumes bearing his name, was eventually able to institute a unification of orthography, albeit not before 1902. His best known reference, *Duden 1 Rechtschreibung* (Orthography), today contains 130,000 words with their spelling variants and rules of usage. The most recent edition contains feminine forms for all professions and trades, some already well established, and others, like *Bundeskanzlerin*, more recently relevant. Of course, it remains to be seen whether the Duden will ever need to add the feminine variant *Päpstin*.

## Defending the language against invasion

The colorful etymologies of the names of the days of the weak (covered in Chapter 8 of this volume) serve to illustrate the German language's connections to other cultures and languages. Currently, there are a number of proposals designed to curb some of that interaction, particularly with regard to the

Anglicization of German. Advertising, marketing and multimedia are among the areas that tend most to use words from English, most of the time purely for convenience. While many of these make sense, a significant number are awkward or even by English standards downright wrong: *Handy*, for example, is an adjective in English referring to the opportune convenience of an object, having nothing to do with its German use as the term for a cellular or mobile telephone. The German term *Wellness* isn't widely used in English; the closest approximation is a *spa*, and even that does not equal the German term, which relates to those things, physical and mental, that one does to achieve and maintain a state of well being.

As English words enter German, they become neologisms, subject to the rules of German word building: *ausgeflippt*, for example, takes the English verb "to flip out", adding a separable prefix *(aus-)* to make it more German yet still meaning "flipped out".

As a culture, Germany has traditionally been resistant to other encroaching cultures, hence the root of the word German, from the Latin *Germania*, referring to the land where the germane, indigenous tribes lived; the Romans occupied Germany but its language and its culture remained essentially what they had been, unlike other lands whose languages became the Romance family. As a result, there has always been a tendency for the language to remain truer to itself, and even in the 17th century there were organized efforts to retain linguistic purity (though at that time, efforts were made to keep French out, not English).

Just as with the spelling reform, heated debates and many letters to editors debate the Anglicization of German. Much like France did in the 1970s and onward to stem the invasion of "franglais", Germany has groups dedicated to replacing Anglicisms with German words, though the government has not gone so far as to establish an equivalent of France's *Académie Française*.

In 2008, the *Gesellschaft für deutsche Sprache* (Society for German Language) conducted a survey on the use of Anglicisms such as *Kids* instead of *Kinder/Jugendliche* (youths), *Event* instead of *Veranstaltung*, *Kongress* or *Feier*, *Meeting* instead of *Treffen* or *Besprechung*, and the ubiquitous *E-Mail*. The population was split three ways: equal parts were for and against with 39% reporting that Anglicisms bothered them, 40% not. 17% said the matter should be decided on a word-by-word basis, while 4% didn't care.

Which begs the question: what consitutes a "German" word?

Signage in airports and rail stations rarely display the word *Auskunft* but instead use *Information*, taken from Latin, as a more internationally recognized word. This serves its purpose in places where one can expect many non-Germans who would not readily understand the word *Auskunft*. Still, in his Zwiebelfisch column on *Spiegel Online*, Bastian Sick has made the point that many Anglicisms provide no such benefit (he points to numerous terms such as *downloaden*, which does nothing to improve upon the German verb *herunterladen* and only confuses people, as they do not know how to put it into the past tenses). Sick argues for inclusion of those, like *Information*, that enrich the German language, but not those that are only there to put on the appearance of being fashionable.

It is not just a matter of personal preference that gives credence to Sick's position; in the summer of 2003, a media services company in Cologne conducted a study of German advertising using English slogans and found that most Germans do not properly understand what the English slogans mean. Of 12 ad campaigns studied, 8 immediately changed their programs to German-language slogans.

### The sun and the earth, the moon and snowflakes – the scientist Johannes Kepler

Much like Leibniz, whom we introduced in the preceding chapter, Johannes Kepler, who lived from 1571 to 1630, was gifted in multiple disciplines. He was an astronomer and an astrologer, a mathematician, theologian, physicist and a philosopher. His calculations and discoveries not only confirmed Copernicus' theories but also directly inspired Newton's theory of universal gravitation.

Though his vision was seriously impaired by smallpox that befell him as a child, he also made significant discoveries in the field of optics explaining how light behaves within the human eye, how myopia functions and how eyeglasses improve vision. He also developed new methods of astronomical observation. Using mathematical models, he acquired specialized knowledge about the planets, their locations and movements, including the elliptical and not circular orbits in which they travel, as described in one of his three Laws of Planetary Motion. In mathematics, Kepler described the basic laws of logarithms; he also invented a gear pump for removing water from underground mines whose basic design is still used today.

He also published his findings on the geometrical symmetry of snowflakes, documenting how they are all unique and yet within each, they are perfectly symmetrical at 60-degree intervals. Kepler's calculations of snowflake density led to what became crystallography, and also formed the basis for encoding theory, an integral part of modern communications technology. He also penned a novel, "Somnium", which described how inhabitants of the Moon might view the movement of the Earth through their sky. Thus, he was also one of the first science fiction writers.

All of these endeavors were driven and supported by Kepler's religious convictions. During his lifetime, astrology was considered a legitimate branch of astronomy that sought to detail the effects of God's universe upon Man's existence, and Kepler's science embodied this conviction. Kepler was a Protestant who studied theology at the University of Tübingen, and during his lifetime, Germany and all regions ruled by the Habsburgs were in constant strife, culminating in the Thirty Years' War (see *Schritte international* Glossary XXL Vol. 3, Chapter 6). His professional life was often thrown into turmoil because of his employers' religious allegiances: because he was Protestant, he was banned from Graz for refusing to convert to Catholicism, and later his alma mater suspected him of being a Calvinist heretic. It is surmised that his fictional speculations on travel to the moon and observations of the Earth contributed to this mistrust as well as to charges of witchcraft against his mother. (In Kepler's novel, his protagonist also consults a demon at one point.) After six years, during which she was incarcerated, Kepler was finally able to win her acquittal, but the imprisonment took its toll on her and she died a year and a half after being set free.

The Thirty Years' War also took its toll on Kepler himself; reigning Catholics put his work under seal, even as he assisted the Catholic General Wallenstein. He died in Regensburg and was buried there but his resting place was lost when Gustavus Adolphus' army destroyed the churchyard.

## Historical Fragments

### Of elephants, merchants and pogroms: the Ashkenazi Jews in Germany

Following the destruction of Jerusalem in 70 A.D. by the Romans, Jews were banned from the immediate area, and though they remained the majority of the population of Palestine for some time afterward, many of the survivors were dispersed, beginning the Jewish diaspora. The earliest known Jewish community in Germany, or Ashkenaz as it was known in Hebrew, was established in Köln (Cologne) in 321, when the Emperor Constantine granted them special rights. Evidence of Jewish presence for the next 500 years is scarce, but upon Charlemagne's ascension as Holy Roman Emperor in 800 he sent Isaac, a Jewish merchant, as an interpreter for two of his ambassadors to Baghdad, where Isaac met Caliph Harun-al-Rashid. The Caliph's gift to Charlemagne upon Isaac's and the ambassadors' return was no small matter indeed: it was an elephant, the first one ever seen so far north.

Later emperors extended privileges to the Jews to cultivate trade and various craftsmen's practices. It is quite possible that Jewish merchants were responsible for all trade with Asia in the Middle Ages. European princes readily availed themselves of Jewish merchants' expertise to fill the coffers of their emerging cities, and by the end of the 10th century, Jewish communities (with an estimated total population at this point of about 20,000) were flourishing on the banks of the Mosel, Rhine, Danube and Elbe rivers. Synagogues, schools, hospitals and cemeteries were well established, and local authorities even allowed Jewish settlements to have their own administrative organs within which rabbis were held in high esteem. Owing to their interaction with Germans and other European cultures, a new common language emerged among the Ashkenazi: Yiddish, which takes its name from the German word *jüdisch*.

What had been more or less peaceful coexistence between Jewish and European communities, despite anti-semitism, ended brutally with the Crusades. In 1096 5,000 Jews in Mainz, Worms and Speyer, all situated along the Rhine, were killed in the first pogrom. Obviously the Crusaders' aims were the conversion of heretics and the acquisition of their wealth. Because of Biblical laws banning the shaving of one's beard and mandating head coverings, Jewish men in particular were always easy to spot. Then, in 1434, the first "yellow spot" on Jewish clothing appeared in the city of Magdeburg, as required by decree. Jews were also forbidden to carry weapons and became vulnerable to attack. Since Christians were forbidden to loan money in exchange for interest paid, Jews regularly extended credit, which enabled more commerce but also created resentment, which was likely the impetus behind further pogroms. With the appearance of the Black Death (plague) throughout Europe, the inability to explain the epidemic gave way to the search for a culprit. Rumors that Jews had poisoned wells and caused the illness led to the massacre of thousands.

Antisemitism in Europe had many roots: superstition, ignorance, fear, xenophobia and the misguided belief that Jews had been responsible for the crucifixion of Jesus. Many German states and cites took to banning Jews from many public areas. Frankfurt erected the first Jewish ghetto in 1460; along a 500-meter stretch where 60 people would normally live, the population eventually swelled to an inhumanely overcrowded 3,000. And yet, Frankfurt was also the home of the Bank of Rothschild. But even as the sons of Mayer Amschel Rothschild were financed by princes from all over Europe, they too were confined to living in the *Judengasse* (Jews Alley).

Nevertheless, Jewish culture flourished and their tradition of education never waned. Moses Mendelssohn was one of the most respected philosophers of the 18th century, yet by mere virtue of his religion, Pastor Johann Melchior Goeze of Hamburg publicly challenged his qualification, given that he did not convert to Christianity. Mendelssohn's friend and fellow Enlightenment thinker Gotthold Ephraim Lessing, himself a theologian, was incensed by Goeze's intolerance. When his patron, the Duke of Braunschweig, forbade him to publicly attack the influential Goeze, Lessing subverted his criticism of intolerance and ignorance by writing for the stage. His drama *Nathan der Weise* (Nathan the Wise) premiered in 1779 and is still performed today, recognized as one of the classics of German drama as well as of Enlightenment thought and tolerance. The hero, Nathan, is based upon Moses Mendelssohn. The centerpiece of the drama, known as the Ring Parable, centers around Nathan's response to the Sultan's question to Nathan, which religion of the Holy Land is the one true religion. Nathan tells the Sultan a tale of a father who loved his three sons so much that he could not choose any one over the others to inherit the ring his family had passed from generation to generation, which made its bearer pleasing before God and mankind, so the father had two perfect copies made. The three sons fought after the father's death until a judge ruled that the sons' behavior should prove who was the heir of the true ring, for if the true ring possessed the power to make its bearer pleasing, surely the ring's power would expose the truth. As an allegory for the three major religions, clearly, the world in Lessing's view had yet to see who had inherited the sole truth that Goeze claimed for Christianity.

Sadly, Lessing's efforts did not stem the growing tide of hatred and intolerance. Anti-semitic sentiment only grew across Europe, and the devastation of the First World War only gave those already so inclined more reason to blame Jews for every misery imaginable. With the Nazis' rise to power in 1933, the history of the Jewish people took yet another tragic turn, even worse than the sacking of Jerusalem.

Hitler's "final solution" led to the murder of over 6 million Jews in Europe, and the near-extermination of the Ashkenazi culture that had arisen in the 1900 years prior. Today, sixty years later, some 100,000 Jews now live in Germany, many having migrated from Eastern Europe.

## Self-Evaluation

**En route**  😃 ☺ 😐

### When listening, I can understand (Hören)

– complex directions: *„Also, du gehst rechts, also Richtung Stadtmitte, immer die Fünffensterstraße entlang bis zum Rathaus.“*
– traffic reports: *„In weiten Teilen Baden-Württenbergs dichter Nebel. Fahren Sie bitte ganz besonders vorsichtig.“*

### In written texts, I can understand (Lesen)

– newspaper texts on current topics: *„Dichter Nebel verhindert Starts und Landungen am Flughafen Köln-Bonn“*
– weather forecasts: *„In der Nacht hört der Regen in Norddeutschland langsam auf.“*
– safety instructions: *„Im Straßenverkehr muss man oft plötzlich bremsen. Deshalb müssen die Bremsen einwandfrei funktionieren.“*
– a to-do list: *„9:00 Uhr Kindergarten, 16:00 Uhr Daniel“*
– un e-mail seeking concrete information: *„Lieber Herr Tsara, im März kann man nie wissen, wie das Wetter wird …“*
– a text with diverse opinions on one subject: *Straßenverkehr: Was nervt Sie dabei am meisten?*

### I can produce the following oral structures (Sprechen)

– give local directions and describe a route: *„Du fährst bis zur nächsten Kreuzung. Da musst du links abbiegen.“*
– reason through something: *„Ich hatte schon zwei Unfälle mit dem Rad. Deshalb fahre ich jetzt immer mit Helm.“*
– recount a personal situation related to a specific topic: *„Also, wenn kein Auto kommt, dann gehe ich schon mal bei Rot über die Ampel.“*

### I can produce the following written texts (Schreiben)

– a text describing an itinerary: *„Du fährst am besten immer die B304 entlang. Du kommst …“*
– an e-mail recommending something: *„Lieber Herr Tsara, im Moment ist es bei uns sehr kalt. Nehmen Sie deshalb …“*

| Kursbuch | Textbook |
|---|---|
| **Seite 48** | **page 48** |
| *der Atlantik (Sg)* | *the Atlantic (ocean)* |
| *Ungarn (Sg)* | *Hungary* |
| *die Welle, -n* | *wave* |
| **Seite 49** | **page 49** |
| *auf·bauen* | *to build, put together* |
| beobachten | to observe |
| erlauben | to allow |
| *das Popkonzert, -e* | *pop concert* |
| verreisen | to leave to travel |
| *wild* | *wild* |
| das Zelt, -e | tent |
| **Seite 50** | **page 50** |
| anstrengend | taxing, strenuous |
| *der Dschungel, –* | *jungle* |
| die Insel, -n | island |
| die Küste, -n | coast |
| *der Sonnenhut, ¨e* | *sun hat* |
| trocken | dry |
| *die Wüste, -n* | *desert* |
| **Seite 51** | **page 51** |
| der Aufenthalt, -e | stay, residency |
| die Aushilfe, -n | help, personnel |
| *der Badestrand, ¨e* | *beach for swimming* |
| *die Bettwäsche (Sg)* | *bed linens* |
| *der Campingplatz, ¨e* | *campground* |
| *entspannen (sich)* | *to relax* |
| *die Erholung (Sg)* | *recovery, complete rest* |
| *familiär* | *familial* |
| die Ferien (Pl) | vacation, holiday |
| *gestellt werden* | *to be provided* |
| das Handtuch, ¨er | hand towel |
| das Huhn, ¨er | chicken |
| die Innenstadt, ¨e | city center |
| *die Kuh, ¨e* | *cow* |
| *das Leihboot, -e* | *loaner boat* |
| *paddeln* | *to paddle* |
| *der Panoramablick (Sg)* | *panoramic view* |
| *das Paradies, -e* | *paradise* |
| *die Region, -en* | *region* |
| das Schwein, -e | pig |
| der Spielplatz, ¨e | playground |
| *stinkend* | *stinking* |
| *der Surfkurs, -e* | *surfing class* |
| *der Tauchkurs, -e* | *diving class* |
| *tierlieb* | *animal-friendly* |

| | |
|---|---|
| die Umgebung (Sg) | surroundings |
| die Unterkunft, ¨e | accomodations |
| *der Waschraum, ¨e* | *laundry room* |
| **Seite 52** | **page 52** |
| *ausgebucht sein* | *to be fully booked* |
| beeilen (sich) | to hurry, rush |
| *der Billigflug, ¨e* | *cheap flight* |
| die Busreise, -n | bus trip |
| *deutschlandweit* | *Germany-wide* |
| *ein·zeichnen* | *to draw in* |
| die Fähre, -n | ferry |
| *die Reiseroute, -n* | *travel route* |
| von ... an | from ... on(ward) |
| weiter·hören | to continue listening |
| **Seite 53** | **page 53** |
| *der Apfelwein (Sg)* | *apple wine* |
| bis bald | see you/talk to you soon |
| *Dänemark (Sg)* | *Denmark* |
| *der Deich, -e* | *dyke* |
| das Fußballstadion, Fußballstadien | soccer stadium |
| *die grüne Soße* | *green sauce* |
| grüßen | to greet |
| *juhu* | *yoo-hoo* |
| *das Museumsufer, –* | *bank of the river lined with museums* |
| *der Umzug, ¨e* | *move (from one home to another)* |
| **Seite 54** | **page 54** |
| *die Abenteuergruppe, -n* | *adventure group* |
| *abenteuerlustig* | *eager for adventure* |
| *der Abenteurer, –* | *adventurer* |
| *Alaska (Sg)* | *Alaska* |
| blond | blond |
| dafür – dagegen sein | to be in favor of/against it |
| *einigen (sich)* | *to come to an agreement* |
| einsam | lonely |
| erholen (sich) | to recover, recuperate |
| *die Erholungsgruppe, -n* | *recuperation group* |
| *faulenzen* | *to laze around, do nothing* |
| *gelaunt* | *in a ... mood* |
| *die Genießerin, -nen* | *female epicure, bon vivant* |
| giftig | poisonous |
| *die Kulturgruppe, -n* | *culture group* |
| die Laune, -n | mood |
| leer | empty |
| mit·nehmen, du nimmst mit, er nimmt mit, er hat mitgenommen | to take along |
| *der Mitreisende, -n* | *fellow traveler* |

| | |
|---|---|
| neugierig | curious |
| der Reisebegleiter, – | travel escort/companion |
| das Risiko, Risiken | risk |
| die Sahara (Sg) | Sahara |
| die Sportgruppe, -n | sports group |
| der Sportsfreund, -e | friend from sports |
| der Sunnyboy, -s | happy, friendly young man who spends a lot of time in the sun |
| die Traumreise, -n | dream trip |
| unkompliziert | uncomplicated |
| die Urlaubsbegleitung, -en | vacation escort |
| der Urlaubstyp, -en | vacation type |
| die Wärme (Sg) | warmth |

## Seite 56 — page 56

| | |
|---|---|
| ab·springen, er ist abgesprungen | to jump out |
| ab·stürzen | to crash |
| der Ballon, -s/-e | balloon |
| die Ballonfahrt, -en | hot air balloon trip |

## Seite 57 — page 57

| | |
|---|---|
| das Argument, -e | argument, case |
| auf·steigen, er ist aufgestiegen | to climb, go up |
| der Ballonflug, ⸚e | balloon flight |
| der Berufspilot, -en | career pilot |
| die Fluggesellschaft, -en | airline |
| der Heißluftballon, -s/-e | hot air balloon |
| der Informatiker, – | computer scientist |
| der IT-Spezialist, -en | IT specialist |
| die Jahreshälfte, -n | half of the year |
| der Kfz-Mechaniker, – | auto mechanic |
| der Krankenpfleger, – | male nurse |
| die Liebe (Sg) | love |
| der Mitspieler, – | fellow player |
| der Passagier, -e | passenger |
| der Rückweg, -e | return, way back |
| der Rundblick | view all the way around |
| die Startvorbereitung, -en | take-off preparation |
| südbayerisch | southern Bavarian |
| das Voralpenland (Sg) | Alpine foothill country |
| das Winterhalbjahr, -e | winter half of the year |

## Arbeitsbuch — Workbook

### Seite 124 — page 124

| | |
|---|---|
| das Urlaubsziel, -e | vacation destination |

### Seite 125 — page 125

| | |
|---|---|
| die Atlantikküste (Sg) | Atlantic coast |

## Seite 126 — page 126

| | |
|---|---|
| puh! | phew! |
| tagsüber | during the day |
| traumhaft | dreamlike |
| die Wanderung, -en | hike |

## Seite 127 — page 127

| | |
|---|---|
| die Freizeitmöglichkeiten (Pl) | here: available free time activities |
| kinderfreundlich | child-friendly |
| kinderlieb | kind to children |
| die Kleinanzeige, -n | classified advertisement |

## Seite 128 — page 128

| | |
|---|---|
| komfortabel | comfortable |

## Seite 129 — page 129

| | |
|---|---|
| die Heimatstadt, ⸚e | hometown, city of one's birth |
| das Kaffeehaus, ⸚er | café (in Vienna) |
| wieder·sehen, du siehst wieder, er sieht wieder, er hat wiedergesehen | to see again |

## Seite 130 — page 130

| | |
|---|---|
| die Ameise, -n | ant |
| das Apartmenthotel, -s | apartment hotel |
| die Ausflugsmöglichkeit, -en | possibility for taking an excursion |
| das Ausflugsziel, -e | excursion destination |
| die Chaussee, -n | avenue, causeway |
| die Kleingruppe, -n | small group |
| das Quellenverzeichnis, -se | source index |
| staunen | to be astonished |
| die Wandzeitung, -en | wall newspaper |
| weise | wise |

## Seite 131 — page 131

| | |
|---|---|
| der Abenteuerurlaub, -e | adventure vacation |
| auf·brechen, du brichst auf, er bricht auf, er ist aufgebrochen | to break out, to head out on a trip |
| der Erholungsurlaub, -e | recuperative vacation |
| der Kulturuurlaub, -e | cultural vacation |
| die Radiodurchsage, -n | radio announcement |
| der Sinn (Sg) | sense, meaning |
| der Sporturlaub, -e | sports vacation |
| der Tenniskurs, -e | tennis course |
| zurück·kehren | to return |

## 1   Locational prepositions (Lokale Präpositionen)

examples | *Letztes Jahr waren wir im Urlaub **im Süden**, dieses Jahr fahren wir mal **in den Norden**.* | Last year we were in the south on vacation. This year, we're driving to the North.

*Wir könnten mal wieder **ans Meer** fahren.* – *Ach nein, **am Meer** waren wir doch schon so oft!*

We could go to the ocean again. – Oh no, We've been on the shore so many times already!

*Ich wäre jetzt gern **auf einer Insel** in der Karibik.* – ***Auf eine Insel** in der Karibik kriegst du mich aber nicht!*

Right now I'd really like to be on an island in the Carribean. – You won't get me on(to) an island in the Caribbean!

In *Schritte international 2*, Chapter 11 you were introduced to the locational prepositions *an*, *in* and *auf (an der Wand, im Bett, auf dem Tisch)*. In this chapter, we will look at an extension of their locational uses. In the context of geographic locations, these three prepositions convey specific spatial relationships:

| | | |
|---|---|---|
| *an* | (on or at, referring to borders where one edge meets another) | *am Strand, an der Küste, am Meer, am See,* (land meeting water) *an der Grenze* (one city, state or other political entity meeting another), *am Horizont* (sky meeting land) |
| *in* | (in) | *im Gebirge, in den Bergen, im Wald* |
| *auf* | (on or at, referring to horizontal surfaces, areas in a city that in medieval times would have been elevated or in a fortress) | *auf einer Insel* (horizontal land above the surrounding water), *auf einem Berg* (the peak or summit), *auf der Post, auf dem Markt* |

Remember that these prepositions require the dative case when they describe a location, and they require accusative case when describing a destination.

**Wo? + dative**

| m | *im Süden* | *am Strand* | *auf einem Berg* |
|---|---|---|---|
| n | *im Gebirge* | *am Meer* | *auf dem Land* |
| f | *in der Wüste* | *an der Küste* | *auf einer Insel* |
| pl | *in den Bergen* | *an den Stränden* | *auf den Inseln* |

**Wohin? + accusative**

| m | *in den Süden* | *an den Strand* | *auf einen Berg* |
|---|---|---|---|
| n | *ins Gebirge* | *ans Meer* | *aufs Land* |
| f | *in die Wüste* | *an die Küste* | *auf die Insel* |
| pl | *in die Berge* | *an die Strände* | *auf die Inseln* |

but: ***nach** Italien, **nach** Rom*

These three prepositions will also contract with articles:

| | |
|---|---|
| *an dem → am* | *an das → ans* |
| *in dem → im* | *in das → ins* |
| | *auf das → aufs* |

# Forms and Structures

**12**

## 2    Adjective declension: zero article *(Adjektivdeklination bei Nullartikel)*

examples

*Wunderschöner Campingplatz in ruhiger Umgebung.*

Fantastic campground in quiet surroundings.

*Kleine Pension mit schönem Blick.*

Small B&B with great view.

German classified ads, like English-language ads, often omit articles to save space (and money on the word count). If adjectives are paired with the nouns in German, they will take endings. Remember how in previous chapters of this volume, we emphasized that if an article docs not show the noun's gender, case and number, the adjective must then do it. The same rule applies for nouns with no article, also called zero article or *Nullartikel*: since there is no article to give that information, the adjective takes on the ending of the definite article.

**nominative**

| | |
|---|---|
| *der Campinglatz* | → *schöner Campingplatz* |
| *das Zimmer* | → *großes Zimmer* |
| *die Pension* | → *kleine Pension* |
| *die Appartments* | → *günstige Appartments* |

**dative**

| | | |
|---|---|---|
| *mit dem Blick* | → *mit schönem Blick* | (compare: *mit einem/dem schönen Blick*) |
| *mit dem Bad* | → *mit modernem Bad* | (compare: *mit einem/dem modernen Bad*) |
| *in der Umgebung* | → *in ruhiger Umgebung* | (compare: *in einer/der ruhigen Umgebung*) |
| *in den Wäldern* | → *in herrlichen Wäldern* | (compare: *in-/den herrlichen Wäldern*) |

**accusative**

| | |
|---|---|
| *den Campingplatz* | → *schönen Campingplatz* |
| *das Zimmer* | → *großes Zimmer* |
| *die Pension* | → *kleine Pension* |
| *die Appartments* | → *günstige Appartments* |

## 3    The preposition *ohne* + accusative *(Präposition „ohne")*

examples

*Ohne seinen Computer fühlt sich Max nicht wohl.*

Without his computer, Max doesn't feel well.

*Natur pur ohne lauten Verkehr.*

Pure nature without loud traffic.

The preposition *ohne* always requires the accusative case. We have already seen this preposition followed by nouns with no article:

*Ich möchte den Kaffee ohne Milch und Zucker.*
*Das Doppelzimmer kostet 70,- € ohne Frühstück.*

### 4   Temporal prepositions *(Temporale Präpositionen)*

**a**   *von ... an* + dative

examples   *Von März **an** fährt der Katamaran täglich.*     From March on, the catamaran goes out daily.
           *Von diesem Jahr **an** gibt es neue Tarife.*     From this year on, there are new prices.

The preposition *von ... an* indicates the onset of a period of time with no set end. The corresponding questions are *Von wann an?* or *Ab wann?*
The time or beginning indicator is found between the two parts of the preposition:

*von heute an*
*von Sonntagmorgen an*
*von 6 Uhr morgens an*

The expression *von .. an* is synonymous with *ab*:

*Ab März fährt der Katamaran täglich. (Von März an ...)*
*Ab diesem Jahr gibt es neue Tarife. (Von diesem Jahr an ...)*

**b**   *über* + accusative

examples   *Sie hat in Hamburg **über** vier Stunden Aufenthalt.*     In Hamburg, she has an over four-hour stay.

           *Die Reparatur hat **über** einen Monat gedauert.*     The repair took over a month.

*Über* has many other meanings besides the locational one. One of those is quantitative, indicating more than a particular amount. This can be used in several contexts; the examples here are temporal. In this context, *über* can substitue for *mehr als*:

*Sie hat in Hamburg mehr als vier Stunden Aufenthalt.*
*Die Reparatur hat mehr als einen Monat gedauert.*

En *Schritte international 2*, Chapters 8 and 12, you've already been introduced to some other prepositions that can answer the question *wann?* and others that answer the question *wie lange?*

*Wann?*
*am Montag (+D)*
*beim Abendessen (+D)*
*vor einer Woche (+D)*
*nach einem Monat (+D)*
*in einem Jahr (+D)*
*um 10 Uhr*
*gegen 10 Uhr* (around 10 o'clock)

*Wie lange?*
*seit einer Stunde (+D)*
*für einen Monat (+A)*
*von Montag bis Freitag (+D, +A)*
*bis nächste Woche (+A)*
*über einen Monat (+A)*

*Ab wann? / Von wann an?*
*ab Montag (+D)*
*von dieser Woche an (+D)*

Most temporal prepositions required the dative case. In this list, *für, bis, um, gegen* and *über* require accusative.

**5** **Translate into English.**

**a** *Fahrt ihr dieses Jahr wieder in die Berge?* .................................................

*– Nein, wir wollen mal an die Küste,* .................................................

*wahrscheinlich an die Ostsee.* .................................................

**b** *Familie Müller zieht um, sie haben sich* .................................................

*ein Haus auf dem Land gekauft.* .................................................

*– Ja, da haben sie auch mehr Ruhe als* .................................................

*in der Stadt.* .................................................

**c** *Dieses Jahr möchte Kurt mal nicht* .................................................

*nur am Strand liegen. Er möchte mal* .................................................

*etwas ganz anderes machen.* .................................................

*– Das kann ich verstehen. Wir machen eine* .................................................

*Fahrt durch die Wüste. Komm doch mit!* .................................................

**6** **Translate into English.**

**a** *Wie lange dauert ein Flug nach Australien?* .................................................

*– Über 20 Stunden.* .................................................

**b** *Frau Kleinfeld, von heute an kümmern Sie* .................................................

*sich bitte wieder um die Sprachkurse.* .................................................

*– Oh, das freut mich aber!* .................................................

**c** *Von elf Uhr abends an fahren* .................................................

*die Busse nicht mehr so oft.* .................................................

*– Ich weiß. Vielleicht kann* .................................................

*ich ja bei Inge mitfahren.* .................................................

**7** **Translate into German.**

**a** On the weekend, we could go back to the .................................................

beach. .................................................

*– Oh no, I get bored at the beach! Why* .................................................

don't we drive to the mountains? .................................................

**b** I go to Lake Constance on vacation. .................................................

I found a lovely B&B with a view of the .................................................

lake. .................................................

**c** Small apartment in quiet area to rent, .................................................

with large terrace & fantastic view. .................................................

**8**   **Translate into German.**

**a** How was the trip? .................................................

– Good, but stressful, too. The flight lasted .................................................

five hours and then we had another hour's *und dann* .................................................

delay. *auch noch* .................................................

**b** Beginning January 1st, busses 21 and 33 .................................................

will also stop at the train station. .............. *halten* ..................

– Do they pass Mozart Square, too? .................................................

**c** I would like to reserve a single room, please. .................................................

– Gladly. This would be for when? ........................................ *wäre das?*

For May 3rd. .................................................

– And for how many nights? .................................................

## Listening and Pronunciation

Up till now, you have learned that the primary stress in a sentence of phrase tends to fall at the end, where the most important information is located.
It is important to note, however, that if another element carries the primary importance in the information being communicated, the primary stress will shift to reflect that.

*auf dem Tisch (nicht hinter dem Tisch)*

In the case of compound nouns, as a general rule the first word in the compound is key to determining the context or meaning of the second word and as a result, that first word in the compound noun will usually get the primary stress.

*Regenschirm, Sonnenschein*

## Familiarity and Understanding

### German emigration

Every week, German television airs a total of 22 hours of programming devoted to reality shows on emigration. It's a very popular current topic. Cameras accompany singles, entire families, au pairs, and others in search of a better life. The programs that air then document their first hours, the voyages, the emigrants' naiveté, ignorance, prejudices, disappointments, hopes and accomplishments. The reasons vary why over 150,000 Germans leave their native land each year nowadays, but for 80% who go, they say that what they want is more likely to be found abroad, and more than half of them complain that Germany is too bureaucratic, taxed too highly, and too pessimistic. Today's emigrants, whether leaving for a few years or for a lifetime, tend to come from the urban areas of western Germany, and they also tend to be highly professionally qualified.

150,000 emigrants constitute an annual loss of 0.2% of the total population, and some experts claim that this number is artificially low; unofficially, some estimate that more than 250,000 leave each year. But the most striking statistic is that 60% more Germans are emigrating than in the 1990s, and this is the highest percentage of emigration in over 120 years.

The preferred destinations are Austria and Switzerland (where 16% go), followed by the United States and Canada (8%), Poland, Great Britain (6%), France and Spain (5%). The drain this places upon Germany's supply of qualified workers is so high that the German government reports shortages in some fields of as many as 50,000 engineers; for the German economy, this translates into a loss of 3.5 billion Euros of income generated. All of this is occurring despite the fact that for decades, Germany was the destination of choice for immigrants, with as many as 80,000 per year entering the country for work.

There were several waves of German emigration in the 19th and 20th centuries. In the early 19th century, bad harvests drove many Germans to areas south-southwest of the Caucasus and to the United States. As Germany transitioned from an agricultural society to a more industrialized one, population growth exploded, and as more people moved to the cities in search of factory work, poverty also increased, launching another wave of emigration to North America. After the First World War, the exodus turned toward South America. Brazil still hosts a region in its south that is home to more than one million German speakers. Emigrants usually sailed from Bremerhaven or Hamburg, and both of these cities have recently opened emigration museums.

None of these earlier waves of emigration share much in common with the forced migrations and exiles that occurred between 1933 and 1945, during the period of the Third Reich, when many fled or were forced out. Hundreds of thousands of Jews, including such prominent individuals as physicist Albert Einstein, writers Stefan Zweig and Elias Cannetti, and filmmaker Billy Wilder fled for their lives. During the Third Reich, numerous artists also emigrated, including poet and dramatist Bertolt Brecht, actress Marlene Dietrich, and the writers Thomas Mann and his brother Heinrich. These are but a few of the names on the long, sad list of those compelled to leave, lest they and their loved ones have suffered the consequences of remaining under Nazi rule.

## Günter Wallraff

The Swedish language has a specific term for doing investigative reporting under an assumed identity: wallraffa.

Günter Wallraff, journalist and author, has become world famous for writing about what one might terms "areas of shame" in German society. In 1983, Wallraff darkened his fair Germanic skin, donned a dark wig and brown contact lenses, and practiced speaking in broken, inflected German so that he could pass for a Turkish *Gastarbeiter* (guest worker) and take menial jobs in various German and multinational companies. He experienced not only the degrading and racist treatment to which Turks in Germany were regularly subjected, but he also gained tremendous insight into a good deal of German corporate noncompliance with employment security, taxation and work safety issues.

"*Ganz unten*" (literally translated: all the way under, known in English by the title "Lowest of the Low") is the title of the book he published describing his experiences. It sold 4 million copies in Germany and was translated into 33 languages. The Turkish edition has sold more than 80,000 copies. This was not Wallraff's first investigative undertaking; in 1977, he took a job at the most widely circulated (and controversial) tabloid paper in Germany, the *BILD-Zeitung,* and documented its lack of due rigor in its journalism, among other things. He has continued to work undercover, most recently passing as a worker in a bread factory with ties to a major supermarket chain, and he published his findings on humiliating treatment of workers and substandard health and safety compliance in *Die ZEIT*. On another occasion, he worked in a call center and exposed their bullying and fraudulent tactics.

As would be expected, Wallraff has been roundly criticized for his methods and his reporting, but libel, privacy invasion and intellectual and corporate property violation suits brought against him have been decided in his favor in the majority of cases. Some members of the Turkish-German community have criticized him for portraying them as victims, and have published a book titled "*Die ganz oben*" (those all the way on top) about successful Turkish entrepreneurs in Germany.

Nevertheless, Wallraff has, time and again, provided a clear image of life among the disenfranchised in Germany, one that would otherwise scarcely be acknowledged.

## Left and right – the German-language press

Following World War II, Germany was initially governed by the four Allied Powers. The Federal Republic, or West Germany, administered by France, Great Britain and the United States, then drafted and ratified its own consitution, known as the *Grundgesetz* or Basic Law, in 1949. During the Allied administration before the Federal Republic was established, the Allied Powers created a licensing policy for newspapers. Rules banning publication of anything sypathetic to or supportive of the Nazi regime were strictly enforced.

The first newspaper to be licensed by the Allies in September of 1945 was *Der Tagesspiegel*, a daily newspaper in Berlin. A few days later, the first issue of the *Süddeutsche Zeitung* appeared.
Axel Springer founded his media empire in 1946, the same year in which *Die ZEIT*, the prestigious national weekly newspaper, first appeared. In 1947, it was followed by the weekly newsmagazine *Der Spiegel*, and in 1949 the *Frankfurter Allgemeine Zeitung*, known as the *Frankfurter Zeitung* until the Nazis banned it, resumed publication.

Like Americans, Germans, Austrians and Swiss who read daily papers favor subscriptions and home delivery. There are outdoor stands in Germany where papers are sold, especially those not available on a subscription basis, but in contrast to the U.S., most of these stands operate on the honor system and it is generally expected and accepted that those taking papers will pay for them. One also has the option in the German-speaking countries very often to purchase tomorrow's morning edition the evening before, as newspaper editors strive to put their editions to bed before the date of publication. In larger cities, newspapers are often available in shops and restaurants, and early editions are most often available at such locations.

Among the papers that are generally not available by subscription are tabloids, publications of the so-called "yellow journalism" variety. Though subscriptions are favored, the highest circulation of any paper in Germany belongs to the *BILD-Zeitung*, a sensationalist tabloid.

One noticable feature of German newspapers is their comparatively large size. The *Frankfurter Allgemeine Zeitung*, for example, measures 80 x 57 cm when fully opened (31.5 x 22.5 inches). To offer some perspective, standard sizes for American newspapers have been (until the recent recession, when costs forced publishers to cut paper size) 60 x 38 cm (23½ by 15 inches) for broadsheet papers, and 38 x 30 cm (15 by 11¾ inches) for tabloids. European papers generally measure 47 x 31.5 cm (18½ by 12¼ inches). German papers tend to have the same sections as American papers, though the arts & culture or lifestyle section in German is called *Feuilleton*. This section usually contains more serious criticism of arts and literature than an American paper, and this cultural engagement is generally taken more seriously by German-language papers than by their American counterparts. The *Süddeutsche Zeitung* has gone so far as to launch its own library of international modern classics (50 important novels of the 20th century) with over 1 million volumes sold for the entire series. This success has been extended to include a DVD library of classic films.

### Süddeutsche Zeitung

The most widely circulated German daily paper is the *Süddeutsche Zeitung*, with more than 400,000 copies each day (as of 2009), and is read by over a million people each day. Though Bavaria tends to be politically conservative, the editorial policy of the *Süddeutsche* is fairly liberal. The *Süddeutsche Zeitung* is circulated throughout Germany but carries a great deal of news specific to Bavaria and Munich. It has an outstanding reputation in the areas of arts and culture coverage as well as in international reporting.

### Frankfurter Allgemeine Zeitung

The *Frankfurter Allgemeine Zeitung*, with a daily run of about 360,000 copies, has the largest circulation abroad, maintains a conservative editorial stance, and in the recent past has been notible for its participation in discussions concerning recent German history. Most notably from 1986 to 1989, the *FAZ* ran coverage of a dispute among German historians on how the Nazi era should be interpreted (*Historikerstreit*).

The *Frankfurter Allgemeine Zeitung* later refused to publish a novel by Martin Walser which, according to the editor of the *Feuilleton*, contained anti-semitic elements. This unleashed a lengthy discussion in the paper of the historical interpretation of the Third Reich. The FAZ also published the first interview with Günter Grass in which the celebrated author and Nobel laureate confessed his brief membership in the SS when he was 16.

### Die ZEIT

Among German print media, the most widely circulated weekly is *die ZEIT* with over 505,000 copies sold and over two million readers each week. Its articles are notoriously in-depth and written for a discering audience. Its entire archive dating back to its 1946 founding is available online free of charge.

### Der Spiegel – Focus – Stern

The weekly magazine *der Spiegel* sells over one million copies every Monday. In addition to its reputation as one of the primary sources for reliable reporting, it also has the distinction of having been news itself on more than one occasion. During what is known as the *Spiegel-Affäre, der Spiegel* published a report indicating that the Bundeswehr and NATO were not capable of defending West Germany from a Soviet attack. Charges of treason were brought against *Spiegel* editors, but the cases were dismissed and members of the Chancellor's cabinet were forced to resign. This incident set a precedent for *der Spiegel* to engage in investigative journalism and to expose serious political and financial scandals. In the 1990s, the magazine's existence was threated financially with the launch of *Focus*, editorially more to the right of *der Spiegel*. Initially, *Focus* cost *der Spiegel* about 10% of its circulation and 12% of its advertising revenue, but *der Spiegel* has since won back this market share. *Focus*, meanwhile, sells about 700,000 copies weekly, about half by subscription.

*Stern*, the other newsweekly, suffered an enormous loss in reader confidence with the 1983 scandal surrounding its publication of Hitler's diaries, which were quickly exposed as forgeries. Still, over 950,000 copies are sold every week.

### BILD

The most commercially successful newspaper in Germany is the *BILD*. Its 3.5 million copies per day far exceeds any other paper. But for its 11 million readers, it is considered more a guilty pleasure than a serious source for news. Often, business commuters are seen reading the *BILD* inside of more respectable papers, and men often claim they only read it for the superior sports coverage.

Like the Fleet Street tabloids of England, the *BILD's* headlines are garish, given to exaggeration, and often geared toward scandal. Naked women are featured on the inside pages. Politically, the *BILD* has always been very conservative; as in all publications of the Axel Springer Verlag, East Germany was always referred to in print as "DDR" (including the quotation marks) to reflect the editorial stance that the German Democratic Republic was a Soviet, not German state and not at all democratic.

The Austrian equivalent of the *BILD* is *Kronenzeitung*. Other larger newspapers in Austria are *die Presse*, the oldest in Austria, and *der Standard, Salzburger Nachrichten* and the *Wiener Zeitung*.

### Neue Zürcher Zeitung

Switzerland's most prestigious newspaper is the *Neue Zürcher Zeitung*. Along with the Austrian *Wiener Zeitung* (founded in 1703) and the German *Hildesheimer Allgemeine Zeitung* (1705) it is the oldest German-language newspaper still in circulation. With its broad coverage of cultural and international affairs, it enjoys an outstanding reputation, and its international version is circulated in Germany as well.

## Historical Fragments

### „*Stadtluft macht frei!*" City air sets you free – on the evolution of cities in the German-speaking countries

Germanic tribes built no cities; theirs were agricultural societies and they lived in small villages rarely exceeding 100 inhabitants. In contrast, Rome at the beginning of the previous millenium had over one million inhabitants, and it was the Romans who founded cities in Germany. Trier, founded by Caesar Augustus and originally named "Augusta Treverorum" is the oldest city in the German-speaking territories. Romans also established the cities of Köln (Cologne), Koblenz, Mainz, Augsburg, Regensburg, and in what is now Switzerland, Kaiseraugst (originally Augusta Raurica), as well as the city of Vindobona in Austria, later known as Wien (Vienna).

The Roman Empire brought Christianity to the region, and the structure of the Church's dioces helped to establish a sort of cultural continuity. This stability however disappeared during the time of the *Völkerwanderung*, or Great Migration, between about 300 and 800 AD. Subsequently, the revitalization of commerce coupled with the defense against outside invaders (Vikings and Magyars) served as the basis for the rise of the Franks' empire in the 9th century (led by Charlemagne). Since most cities were located along important trade routes, merchants and tradesmen were clustered there as well. As we saw in the previous chapter of this volume, alliances such as the Hansa took root under such conditions.

After 1100, the western European population grew considerably with the advent of improved agricultural practices and clearing of forests for more planting area. Between 1000 and 1250, the percentage of land that was forested decreased from 90 to 20%. Crowding created conditions whereby many Germans began to settle in Slavic territories east of the Elbe and Danube rivers, assimilating into the existing populations. Thus arose new cities east of the Empire, extending the influence of both the Emperor and the Church as well as that of the nearest local sovereign. This "colonization of the East" continued through the 14th century and was a major driving force behind the Christianization of the Nordic countries (via Bremen and Hamburg) and the eastern, Slavic lands. (The latter refers to the spread of Roman Catholicism; many areas of Eastern Europe had been Orthodox Christian for centuries before Western Europe was converted).

One important means of attracting new citizens to these cities was the concept of the *"freie Stadt"* or the Free City, also known as the Independent City. Not only was the City itself free of many restrictions that would otherwise be imposed by outside authority, but peasants who otherwise would spend their lives essentially enslaved in feudal agricultural or military work could earn their freedom from their landlord simply by managing to stay within a free city for one year and one day. "Stadtluft macht frei", city air makes you free, was the saying that arose in the 11th century in reference to this law.

Other cities achieved military and political freedom, such as Lübeck, the powerful capital of the Hansa. There were other cities who were dependent upon a local sovereign (such as Berlin) and others who answered only to the Emperor, such as Hamburg, Bremen, Nürnberg (Nuremberg) and Köln (Cologne). Surrounding areas were dependent upon these cities, who were able to issue their own currency and manage their own customs, financial and military services. The latter was most often evinced by the fortifying walls built around the cities. Any man capable of work was obligated to aid in the defense of the city.

Medieval cities were ruled by patricians whose wealth came from their foreign trade and their income as landlords beyond the city walls. Craftsmen were united in guilds and were able to set fixed prices for their work as well as the number of those practicing their trades. The lowest social strata, however, had no voice and no power.

At the beginning of the modern age, 115 cities remained sovereign and free, but by the end of the Thirty Years' War and after further political developments such as Napoleon's Mediatization in 1803, only four remained. Today, three *Länder* carry the designation of Free City (and thus of city-states within the Federal Republic): Hamburg, Bremen and Berlin.

## Self-Evaluation

**Trips and Travels**

### When listening, I can understand (Hören)

– a conversation at a travel agency: *„Wann wollen Sie denn fliegen?"* – *„Am 15. September."* – *„Oh, das tut mir leid, aber …"*
– announcements and information on the radio: *„Autofahrer auf der Autobahn zwischen München und Lindau. Achtung, es gibt …"*

### In written texts, I can understand (Lesen)

– interviews about hobbies: *Eine runde Sache*
– advertisements in travel brochures: *Wunderschöner Campingplatz in ruhiger Umgebung. Nur fünf Minuten zum Strand.*
– descriptions of places and cities in a letter: *„Unser Haus liegt außerhalb von Bredstedt, nahe an der Grenze zu Dänemark."*
– short magazine or newspaper articles about travel: *Mit dem Fahrrad um die ganze Welt*

### I can produce the following oral structures (Sprechen)

– talk about travel destinations, plan a trip, and book one with an agency: *„Wir könnten in die Sahara fahren." / „Ich möchte eine Reise nach … buchen." / „Wie lange dauert denn der Flug?"*
- talk about my choice of accomodations and justify my choice*: „Also, die Pension im Zentrum liegt sehr günstig …"*

### I can produce the following written texts (Schreiben)

– a letter of invitation to my city, including suggestions for activities: *„Liebe Eva, komm doch mal nach Essen …"*
- a classified ad for vacation lodging: *Familienfreundlicher, großer Bauernhof mit Kühen …*
- a narrative of a trip (real or imagined): *„Ich war schon einmal an der Nordsee."*

# Vocabulary

| Kursbuch | Textbook |
|---|---|
| **Seite 58** | **page 58** |
| ab·heben, er hat abgehoben | to withdraw (money) |
| die EC-Karte, -n | EC Card (debit card) |
| *die Geheimzahl, -en* | *secret number (PIN)* |
| der Geldautomat, -en | ATM, automated teller machine |
| kaputt machen | to break, render useless |
| die Kreditkarte, -n | credit card |
| *die Kundenkarte, -n* | *customer card* |
| *die persönliche Identifikations-nummer, -n (PIN)* | *PIN (personal identification number)* |
| die Telefonkarte, -n | telephone card |
| *vernichten* | *to destroy* |

| **Seite 59** | **page 59** |
|---|---|
| *auswendig lernen* | *to commit to memory* |
| *der Bankschalter, –* | *bank counter* |
| enttäuscht | disappointed |

| **Seite 60** | **page 60** |
|---|---|
| *das Antwortkärtchen, –* | *answer card* |
| *ein·prägen (sich)* | *to imprint* |
| *das Fragekärtchen, –* | *question card* |
| das Konto, Konten | account |
| *das Partnersuchspiel, -e* | *game to find a partner* |
| *die Service-Nummer, -n* | *service (telephone) number* |
| weiter·fragen | to continue asking |
| wieder·bekommen, er hat wiederbekommen | to receive again |

| **Seite 61** | **page 61** |
|---|---|
| *akzeptieren* | *to accept* |
| *die Bankverbindung, -en* | *bank routing and account numbers* |
| *die Bankleitzahl, -en* | *bank routing number* |
| bar | in cash |
| das Bargeld (Sg) | cash |
| der Geldschein, -e | currency note |
| die Kontonummer, -n | account number |
| *die Münze, -n* | *coin* |
| ob | whether |
| überweisen, er hat überwiesen | to transfer |
| *die Ware, -n* | *ware, goods* |
| der Zoll, ¨e | customs |
| der Zins, -en | interest (charged or earned) |

| **Seite 62** | **page 62** |
|---|---|
| *aus·kennen (sich), er hat sich ausgekannt* | *to know one's way around something* |
| *aus·zahlen* | *to pay out* |
| die Einkaufstüte, -n | shopping bag |
| *die Geheimnummer, -n* | *secret number (PIN)* |
| installieren | to install |
| *der Internetzugang, ¨e* | *internet access* |
| nähen | to sew |
| renovieren | to renovate |
| *zu·schicken* | *to send (to someone)* |

| **Seite 63** | **page 63** |
|---|---|
| auf·hören | to stop doing, quit doing |
| *der Berater, –* | *advisor* |
| die Chance, -n | chance, possibility |
| der Gewinn, -e | profit |
| irgend- | any |
| *der Lottogewinn, -e* | *lottery winnings* |
| *der Lottogewinner, –* | *lottery winner* |
| *der Lottoschein, -e* | *lottery ticket* |
| *die Lottozahl, -en* | *lottery number* |
| malen | to paint |
| die Organisation, -en | organization |
| die Rente, -n | retirement |
| *riesig* | *gigantic* |
| *spenden* | *to donate* |
| *und zwar* | *by that, meaning* |
| die Weltreise, -n | trip around the world |
| *die Ziehung, -en* | *pulling, drawing* |
| die Zukunft (Sg) | future |

| **Seite 64** | **page 64** |
|---|---|
| *ab·buchen* | *to debit, charge off* |
| *der Alptraum, ¨e* | *nightmare* |
| das Ausweispapier, -e | identification paper |
| *der Bankmitarbeiter, –* | *bank colleague* |
| *der Biergarten, ¨* | *beer garden* |
| *das Butterbrot, -e* | *slice of bread with butter* |
| ein·zahlen | to deposit, pay in |
| *elektronisch* | *electronic* |
| *erstaunlich* | *astounding* |
| *das Extra-Papier, -e* | *extra (piece of) paper* |
| *das Fahrzeugpapier, -e* | *vehicle document* |
| *der Fingerabdruck, ¨e* | *fingerprint* |
| *die Geldkarte, -n* | *ATM card* |
| *hinein·werfen, du wirfst hinein, er wirft hinein, er hat hineingeworfen* | *to toss in* |
| *der Joghurtbecher, –* | *yogurt container* |

# 13 Vocabulary

| das Kissen, – | pillow |
|---|---|
| die Kopie, -n | copy |
| kopieren | to copy |
| *die Krankenkassenkarte, -n* | *medical insurance card* |
| *die Notfall-Rufnummer, -n* | *emergency services phone number* |
| das Original, -e | original |
| *die Panik (Sg)* | *panic* |
| Prost | cheers |
| *sämtliche* | *complete, collected* |
| der Schein, -e | certificate |
| *der Silvesterknaller, –* | *New Year's noisemaker* |
| *sowie* | *as well as* |
| *das Vermischte* | *assorted (items)* |
| *der Zeigefinger, –* | *index finger* |

## Seite 65 — page 65

| *das Fragepronomen, -pronomina* | *interrogative pronoun* |
|---|---|
| *die indirekte Frage, -n* | *indirect question* |
| *sichern* | *to ensure* |
| *unbestimmt* | *indefinite* |
| *die Unkenntnis (Sg)* | *lack of knowledge* |
| *die Zahlungsmöglichkeit, -en* | *methods of payment* |

## Seite 66 — page 66

| *die Kinderhilfe (Sg)* | *children's aid* |
|---|---|
| *der Passant, -en* | *passerby* |
| *der Räuber, –* | *robber* |

## Seite 67 — page 67

| *das Manuskript, -e* | *manuscript* |
|---|---|
| *die Parkgebühr, -en* | *parking fee* |

## Arbeitsbuch — Workbook

## Seite 134 — page 134

| *an·schließen, er hat angeschlossen* | *here: to connect* |
|---|---|
| bloß | (modal particle) here: the heck, on earth |
| *die Computerabteilung, -en* | *computer department* |

## Seite 137 — page 137

| *die Eisdiele, -n* | *ice cream parlor* |
|---|---|

## Seite 138 — page 138

| *die Gartenbank, ⁺e* | *garden bench* |
|---|---|
| *die Gartenmöbel (Pl)* | *garden furniture* |

## Seite 139 — page 139

| *der Fuchs, ⁺e* | *fox* |
|---|---|
| *gackern* | *to cackle, cluck* |
| *die Gans, ⁺e* | *goose* |
| *der Hahn, ⁺e* | *chicken* |
| der Hausschlüssel, – | house key |
| *schlau* | *clever* |
| das Sportfest, -e | sports festival |
| *der Teich, -e* | *pond* |

## Seite 140 — page 140

| auf·geben, du gibst auf, er gibt auf, er hat aufgegeben | to give up, quit |
|---|---|
| *die Beerdigung, -en* | *burial* |
| *das Chatforum, -foren* | *chat forum* |
| der Fußballklub, -s | football club/soccer club |
| *der Klubpräsident, -en* | *club president* |
| *der Lebenstraum, ⁺e* | *life's dream* |
| *der Reichtum (Sg)* | *riches* |
| der Sportplatz, ⁺e | sports park, outdoor facility |
| das Urlaubsfoto, -s | vacation photo |

## Seite 141 — page 141

| *der Antrag, ⁺e* | *proposal, request, application* |
|---|---|
| *die Entwicklungsabteilung, -en* | *development department* |
| *das Girokonto, -konten* | *checking account* |
| *die Ingenieurwissenschaften (Pl)* | *engineering sciences* |
| *der Lebenslauf, ⁺e* | *résumé* |
| mit·teilen | to communicate, inform |
| *die Rufnummer, -n* | *telephone number* |
| *unter·bringen, er hat untergebracht* | *to house, put up* |
| die Vorwahl, -en | area code |
| *das Wohnheim, -e* | *residencex* |

# Forms and Structures

## 1    Indirect questions with *wer, was ...* *(Indirekte Frage mit „wer, wo, was")*

examples    *Was heißt das?*                   What does that mean?
*Können Sie mir sagen, **was** das **heißt**?*    Can you tell me what that means?

*Wo sind die Toiletten?*              Where are the restrooms?
*Wissen Sie, **wo** die Toiletten **sind**?*    Do you know where the restrooms are?

*Wer sitzt hier?*                    Who's sitting here?
*Weißt du, **wer** hier **sitzt**?*         Do you know who is sitting here?

Instead of asking a question directly, it is often gentler or easier to approach strangers with an indirect question. Both English and German take a similar approach to this construction, though German word order requires a slightly different structure.

In contrast to a direct question where the verb comes before the subject, the indirect question puts the core of the question into a dependent clause, where the interrogative functions as a subordinating conjunction and the conjugated verb moves to the final position.

## 2    Indirect questions with *ob* *(Indirekte Frage mit „ob")*

examples    *Sitzt hier jemand? – Ja. / Nein.*      Is someone sitting here – No. / Yes.
*Weißt du, **ob** hier jemand **sitzt**?*    Do you know if (whether) anyone is sitting here?

For questions that can be answered with *ja/nein*, questions that use no interrogative pronoun such *wer*, *wie*, *was* etc., the conjunction *ob* is used to create an indirect question. In English, *ob* correlates to "if" but **only** in the sense of "whether or not". It does **not** correspond to the conditional "if", which in German is *wenn*.

## 3    The verb: *lassen (Verb: Konjugation)*

examples    *Peter **lässt** das Auto **reparieren**.*    Peter is having the car repaired.
*Ich **lasse** die Pakete **abholen**.*       I'm having the packages picked up.

The verb *lassen* + infinitive makes clear that the subject is not doing the action but has instead given it to someone else to do. It has the same sense as the English construction "to have something done". Note however, that German uses *lassen* as the auxiliary and never *haben* (which is only an auxiliary for the *Perfekt*).

examples    *Wir lassen die Wohnung renovieren.*    We're having the apartment renovated.

*Ich gehe zum Frisör und lasse mir die*    I'm going to the hairdresser and
*Haare schneiden.*                       getting my hair cut.

In English, "having or getting something done" involves a past participle, but in German, it uses the infinitive, which of course comes in the final position.

*Ich **lasse** mir eine neue Karte **ausstellen**.*    I'm having a new card issued.
     2                  final
    conjugated verb     infinitive

As you can see in these examples, then, the verb *lassen* functions exactly the same as the modal verbs do: the conjugated form of *lassen* sits in second position and the infinitive goes to the end.

Ich **muss** mir eine neue Karte **ausstellen lassen**.    I have to get a new card issued.
2                                              final
conjugated verb                     double infinitive

*lassen* + infinitive can also be combined with another modal. In this case, the modal verb is conjugated and goes to second position, while both *lassen* and the other verb appear as infinitives, with *lassen* coming after the other verb.

*lassen* is a strong verb and follows the same pattern as *schlafen*, with a vowel change from *a* to *ä* in the 2nd and 3rd person singular forms.

| singular | plural |
|---|---|
| *ich lasse* | *wir lassen* |
| *du lässt* | *ihr lasst* |
| *er/es/sie lässt* | *sie lassen* |

**4**   **Translate into English.**

**a**   *Ich kenne das Wort Bankleitzahl nicht.*   .............................................................................

*Kannst du mir sagen, was das heißt?*   .............................................................................

*– Tut mir leid, das weiß ich auch nicht.*   ...........................................................

**b**   *Entschuldigung, wissen Sie, wo der Bus*   .............................................................................

*nach Ismaning abfährt?*   .............................................................................

*– Ja, gegenüber dem Bahnhof.*   .............................................................................

**c**   *Weißt du, ob wir die Übung 5 auch machen*   ...............................................................

*sollen?*   .............................................................................

*– Ja, die sollen wir auch machen.*   .............................................................................

**d**   *Ich habe vergessen, wie man das anschließt.*   ...............................................................

*Kannst du mir helfen?*   .............................................................................

*– Ich weiß auch nicht, ob ich das kann.*   .............................................................................

**5**   **Translate into English.**

**a**   *Ich habe meinen Personalausweis verloren.*   ...............................................................

*– Dann musst du dir einen neuen ausstellen*   ...............................................................

*lassen.*   .............................................................................

**b**   *Du musst den Anzug mal reinigen lassen.*   ...............................................................

*– Ja stimmt, kannst du ihn morgen in die*   ...............................................................

*Reinigung bringen?*   .............................................................................

<u>c</u> *Lassen Sie sich im Sekretariat ein Formular* .............................................................

*geben und füllen Sie es aus.* .............................................................

*– Was für ein Formular brauche ich denn?* .............................................................

## 6 Translate into German.

<u>a</u> Excuse me, can you tell me where lecture ..................... *du* .....................

hall 10 is? .............................................................

– Yes, it's the third door on the right. .............................................................

<u>b</u> I don't know anymore if we have class ............... *weiß nicht mehr* ...............

tomorrow. .............................................................

– Yes, till one. .............................................................

<u>c</u> Excuse me, can you tell me how to get to ..................... *sie* .....................

the train station? .............................................................

– Sorry, I'm not from around here. .............................................................

<u>d</u> I don't know if I should give them my .............................................................

e-mail address. ...................................................... *soll.*

– I don't think that's a problem. .............................................................

## 7 Translate into German.

<u>a</u> I'm taking the car to the shop tomorrow. .............................................................

I have to get the oil changed. .............................................................

<u>b</u> I'd like to have these papers translated. .............................................................

Do you know anyone? .............................................................

– My sister does translations. .............................................................

<u>c</u> Where are you going? .............................................................

– To the hairdresser. I want to get my .............................................................

hair cut. .............................................................

## Listening and Pronunciation

In *Schritte international 1*, Chapters 2 and 3, you had your first exposure to what Germans call *Sprechmelodie*, the rise and fall of intonation in a sentence.
In particular, you will recall that closed, or *ja/nein* questions, usually intone up at the end, while open questions, or questions beginning with an interrogative, intone downward.

When questions become indirect, however, those patterns can and often do change. Take, for example, this indirect question:

*Weißt du schon* →, *wann du kommst?* ↗

If this had been a direct question (*Wann kommst du?*) it would have intoned down.
However, the first part of the question is a closed question in itself, so the intonation goes up at the end, even as the first part of the question remains level.

If an indirect question is framed as a command, then the intonation will be level in the first clause, down in the second.

*Sag mir bitte* →, *wo wir uns treffen.* ↘

Though a closed direct question would intone up (*Hast du Hunger?* ↗), placing that same question in an indirect form will change so that the first part remains level, while the second part, the clause beginning with *ob*, intones downward.

*Ich frage dich* →, *ob du Hunger hast.* ↘

## Familiarity and Understanding

### The reign of silence

Imagine if you can a place in the western world devoid of movement, music, and human voices. Imagine a place of complete silence. Such a place exists in some of the cars of the Swiss Federal Rail (*Schweizer Bundesbahn*).
Someone unaccustomed with this particular facet of the Swiss Rail wrote that he sat with someone in one of the compartments where silence is mandated and began to talk quietly. When the conductor came to check tickets, he pointed out that passengers in these areas were forbidden to speak, even in a low voice. So strict is the silence that passengers cannot even listen to MP3 players with headphones, watch videos, or even have cell phones on.
These silent zones function as an island of calm in both first and second class, allowing passengers to work in silence or even just to take in the scenery passing by.
German trains also offer silent compartments, but the rules are not as restrictive on the German Rail, stating instead that noise should be avoided.

Swiss train signage

Signage in some German train compartments, more permissive

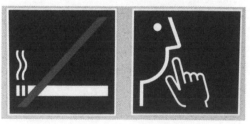

## No aesthetics without ethics

700 m² (7537 sq. ft.), chandeliers, pillars and richly papered walls, distinctive furniture, a garden in the background: certainly, mansions and villas of the rich and famous fit this description. But the particular property in question here is a homeless shelter, remodeled by a German artist who transformed a small house in the Schöneberg section of Berlin into a luxury palace for those who have no home.
Where before there were cold and desolate florescent lights and gray, dirty walls, there are now warm colors and lighting, inviting rooms and beauty everywhere.

Conceptual artist Miriam Kilali (born 1966), is convinced that aesthetic beauty functions to raise morale and to restore a sense of life. Her remodeling project cost 130,000 Euros and was financed by private and public donations. The house was owned and is now operated by the *Diakonisches Werk*, the Protestant charitable organization. Half of the 21 residents (all males with addiction illnesses) are considered permanent residents, but it is Kilali's hope that even they will be reintegrated into society as soon as possible. Residents of the home, known as *Reichtum 2*, (Wealth 2) are involved in ongoing renovation work in the building inasmuch as they are able and are expected to live according to strict rules, including no violence and no hard liquor. The individual rooms are modest in comparison to the common areas but they still have a pleasant atmosphere. The entire concept challenges the dominant belief that housing for the homeless should be "appropriate" to their milieu.

Kilali's Berlin project followed the success of *Reichtum 1* in Moscow, Russia. She does not want these two projects to be the only ones, as she sees no reason why the rest of our world should not also be beautified. What they have accomplished in these homes, she says, can also be applied to playgrounds and hospitals. Kilali originally trained as a dressmaker, then studied art and worked at a shelter in the Berlin district of Kreuzberg. Always deeply affected by the desperation of the people there, she knew that the creation of art could help to break the paralyzing effect of poverty. For her, it was clear that she could do something with art: "From my own experience, I knew that it was a beautiful force. And anyone who has lived on the street knows this twice as well."

## The fatal consequences of the ink on Bach's scores

Composer Johann Sebastian Bach lived about three hundred years ago, from 1685 to 1750. He was a prodigious composer who continues to influence music composers and performers around the world even today. Indeed, more of his music is included on the sound recordings sent into outer space on the Voyager probes than that of any other composer.

Bach composed using black ink. Since Antiquity, ink such as that which Bach used was composed of three principal ingredients: gall nut extract, gum arabic and iron sulfate. Known as iron gall ink, it had been favored over carbon-based (i.e., plant-based) inks because not only was it darker, but the ink held deeply to the paper and was essentially indelible. But what no one could know at the time was that in holding so fast to the paper, iron gall ink was actually corroding the paper. For a composer such as Bach, who continually revised his scores, wrote in the margins and often on both sides of a sheet, there was that much more ink going into the paper – and slowly destroying his scores.

This unfortunate conflagration of contributing factors led to a tragedy in cultural preservation and a nightmare for paper conservators. Between the high level of iron sulfate in his inks and the lower grade of paper that Bach used (his came from northern Germany, while Mozart and Haydn, for example, used better quality paper from Italy which deteriorates more slowly) there has already been complete oxidation in some points of the scores. Furthermore, when exposed to air and humidity, the iron sulfate decomposes into sulfuric acid, a chemically aggressive substance. Where once there was a quarter note, for example, there is now just a hole in the paper. In time, this natural chemical progression would render all of his scores illegible, even reducing them to dust. In many respects, the progression of this deterioration almost seems to have a romantic effect, soaking the notes through the paper. But in areas where Bach wrote semiquavers and other intricate notations, the notes are literally falling through the paper and away.

Even in the late 19th century, conservators were concerned about the *Tintenfraß* (literally, the ink's gobbling up of the paper) and held a research conference in St. Gallen, Switzerland on the topic. Several attempts had been made to save the manuscripts, and as was the case in so many other matters, the division of Germany greatly hindered progress toward a solution. In the 1990s in Leipzig (the city where Bach spent most of his life), the procedure was finally developed, building upon findings from the 19th century, to use gelatin release papers to split each sheet (separating front from back) and insert a highly alkaline neutralizing "core sheet" between them, then reattach the sheet halves. An enzymatic bath then dissolves the gelatin of the release papers, freeing the original document with its stabilizing core intact. Between 2000 and 2003, 3,579 sheets of Bach's scores were restored using this *Papierspaltverfahren* (paper splitting process), at enormous cost. 1.8 million Euros were contributed by 1100 private donors worldwide, while the balance came from the *Deutsche Forschungsgemeinschaft* (German Research Society) and from the *Bundesverwaltungsamt/Zivilschutz* (Federal Administration/Civil Defense).

Using the term "restored" is a bit misleading; what was destroyed by the *Tintenfraß* can never be brought back. For now, though, the damage has been halted and slowed to an immeasurable crawl. Bach's scores also have a new home. In the past, the papers were stuffed into envelopes made of acidic paper and stacked tightly on shelves, only intensifying the disintegration. The holdings of the Bach Collection at the *Staatsbibliothek zu Berlin* (Berlin State Library), which constitute 80% of all Bach manuscripts still in existence, are now stored in acid-free boxes inside alarm-equipped steel vaults with a constant temperature of 18° C (64.4° F) and 50 to 55% relative humidity, shielded from damaging light.

Beginning in 1997, the *Staatsbibliothek* also began a digital imaging process of their Bach holdings, not only as insurance should the *Papierspaltverfahren* not work as planned, but also to make the scores available for wider study, ensuring that Bach will continue to inspire and amaze for generations to come.

## Historical Fragments

### The Emperor and the Pope in the Middle Ages – the origins of the division of Germany

Amid the upheaval of the *Völkerwanderung*, the Church and the Pope managed to maintain a balance of state and municipal administration, and in the role of Bishop of Rome, the Pope also served as the political sovereign of the city during the periods when the city was repeatedly destroyed (410, 455, 536–546).

After the fall of the Roman Empire in 476, the Pope declared the "Patrimonium Sancti Petri" indicating that the Church would rule over its followers as a state church, but the Empire essentially ceased to exist in any tangible form in Western Europe. In its place, the Carolingian Kingdom, also known as the Kingdom of the Franks, arose and filled this power vacuum. In 754, the Franks' king Pépin the Short, (known in German as *Pippin der Erste*) took Rome under the Franks' protection in the Church's conflict with the Lombards of what is now Italy. In exchange, Pope Stephen II recognized the legitimacy of the Franks' rule. In 774, Pépin's successor, his son Charlemagne, had defeated the Lombards and was crowned their king as well. The alliance between the Franks and the Church was further cemented in AD 800 when Pope Leo III crowned Charlemagne Emperor of Rome.

The Carolingian Empire was divided in 843, and again in 870, due to conflicts between heirs to the throne. Following these divisions, however, almost all the German-speaking territories were united under one kingdom in the East. The word *deutsch* originates from the Latin "theodiscus" (language of the people) denoting the common language of the Eastern Frankish Kingdom (also known in English as East Francia), but generally speaking, the language was all the territory shared.

Having defeated the Magyars (Hungarians) in 955, Otto I became the most powerful sovereign of his time as King of Germany, King of Burgundy (in modern-day France) and King of Lombardy. In 962 he was then crowned Emperor of the Holy Roman Empire, which was intended to reestablish the Roman Empire across Europe under the Church's direction. Though the Empire existed through to 1806, it was continually plagued with strife between the Holy See and the Emperor. In the case of Otto I, he sought to strengthen his political position by appointing and giving more power to bishops and abbots, thus giving him more support within the Church possibly against the Pope, and also undermining the authority of the princes beneath him. For his part, Otto I was never able to truly gain an upper hand against the Papacy (though he did succeed in deposing one Pope), and future Emperors faced the same struggle.

In 1122, the Concordat of Worms ended the German Emperors' ability to invest bishops, effectively relinquishing the power within the Church that Otto I had established. As the Emperor could no longer appoint bishops, he could no longer rely on their allegiance. Where bishops had been administrators in the Empire, they were now reduced to the level of vassals and could no longer carry out the Emperor's policies in his absence, thus giving power back to local rulers. Only after a bishop's death could the Emperor name a successor.

In 1356, the Golden Bull Decree of the Imperial Reichstag in Nuremburg set practices of succession in the Empire for 400 years to follow. Seven *Kurfürsten*, or prince-electors, were named whose kingdoms were declared indivisible, and only these seven had the right to elect an Emperor by a simple majority.

Many decades later there were attempts during the reigns of Maximilian I and Charles I to strengthen the central power of the Empire, but all failed. The religious wars following the Protestant Reformation further eroded the Empire, this time as much from a religious standpoint as from a political one. The Thirty Years' War from 1618 to 1648 and the Treaty of Westphalia (see *Schritte international* Glossary XXL, Vol. 3, Chapter 6) left in their wake a land torn asunder, millions dead, and an Emperor stripped of power.

## Self-Evaluation

**Money**      😃 🙂 😐

### When listening, I can understand (Hören)

- conversations on different methods of payment for purchases: *„Ich wollte fragen, akzeptieren Sie auch Kreditkarten?"* – *„Nein, tut mir leid, wir nehmen hier keine Karten, hier können Sie nur bar bezahlen."*
- the lottery drawing numbers as reported on the radio: *Ziehung der Lottozahlen*
- economic advice given to lottery winners by a radio interview guest: *„Viele Lottogewinner können gar nicht glauben, dass sie gewonnen haben."*

### In written texts, I can understand (Lesen)

- texts in magazines or newspapers relating to money (documentation, ATMs, methods of payment): *Der Geldautomat gibt nicht nur Geld, sondern er nimmt es auch.*
- documents needed for applying for employment: *Lebenslauf, Bewerbungsbrief, Visitenkarte*

### I can produce the following oral structures (Sprechen)

- ask about possible payment methods: *„Ich wollte fragen, ob Sie auch Kreditkarten akzeptieren."*
- talk about distinct professional activities: *„Reparierst du dein Fahrrad selbst oder lässt du es reparieren?"*
- talk about a fictitious or hypothetical situation: *„Wie würde Ihr Leben als Lottogewinner aussehen?"*

### I can produce the following written texts (Schreiben)

- a comment on an online forum: *„Das finde ich gut. Man sollte auch als Lottogewinner normal weiterleben."*
- complete forms with appropriate personal data: *Wohnort, …*

| Kursbuch | Textbook |
|---|---|

## Seite 68 — page 68

| die Lebensstation, -en | stage of life |

## Seite 69 — page 69

| der Lieblingsname, -n | favorite name |

## Seite 70 — page 70

| auf·wachsen, du wächst auf, er wächst auf, er ist aufgewachsen | to grow up |
| das Bauernbrot, -e | farmhouse/coarse rye bread |
| die Baustelle, -n | construction site |
| das Dorf, ¨er | village |
| die Energie, -n | energy |
| die Erdbeermarmelade, -n | strawberry marmalade |
| fallen, du fällst, er fällt, er ist gefallen | to fall |
| groß werden, du wirst groß, er wird groß, er ist groß geworden | to become large, grow up |
| die Kindheit (Sg) | childhood |
| die Kindheitserinnerung, -en | childhood memory |
| der Krieg, -e | war |
| die Kuhmilch (Sg) | cow's milk |
| der Lebensmittelladen, ¨ | grocery store |
| das Loch, ¨er | hole |
| mit·helfen, du hilfst mit, er hilft mit, er hat geholfen | to help (with something) |
| die Operation, -en | operation |
| pensioniert | retired |
| die Präteritumform, -en | preterite/simple past form |
| die Seife, -n | soap |
| der Stall, ¨e | stall, (barn) |
| der Tod (Sg) | death |
| die Urgroßtante, -n | great-great-aunt |
| wochenlang | for weeks, lasting for weeks |

## Seite 71 — page 71

| der Comic, -s | comic (book) |
| der Gedanke, -n | thought |
| der Liebeskummer (Sg) | heartbreak |
| die Problemkarte, -n | problem card |
| die Ratschlagskarte, -n | suggestion card |
| die Vorschlagskarte, -n | suggestion card |

## Seite 72 — page 72

| an·sprechen, du sprichst an, er spricht an, er hat angesprochen | to speak to, address |

| der Arbeitskollege, -n | work colleague |
| der Bär, -en | bear |
| das Bärchen, – | little bear |
| der Bereich, -e | area |
| das Dampfmaschinchen, – | little steam machine |
| dankbar | thankful |
| das Dickerchen, – | little tubby/chubby one (affectionate) |
| die Eigenschaft, -en | quality, characteristic |
| der Einfall, ¨e | idea, inspiration |
| einfallslos | lacking in new ideas |
| empfinden, er hat empfunden | to perceive |
| der Engel, – | angel |
| das Engelchen, – | little angel |
| der Esel, – | donkey, ass |
| die Fantasie, -n | imagination |
| das Häschen, – | little rabbit |
| das Häuschen, – | little house |
| der Keks, -e | cookie |
| der Kosename, -n | pet name |
| Mausi | little mouse |
| das Nüdelchen, – | little noodle |
| populär | popular |
| die Privatsache, -n | personal matter |
| der Raucher, – | smoker |
| rein | pure, purely |
| respektlos | disrespectful |
| der Schatz, ¨e | treasure |
| das Schätzchen, – | little treasure |
| das Schwesterchen, – | sister (diminutive) |
| die Wahl, -en | choice |
| die Zuckermaus, ¨e | sugar mouse |
| die Tierwelt (Sg) | animal kingdom |

## Seite 73 — page 73

| die Aufmerksamkeit, -en | attention, notice |
| dazu gehören | to belong to that, be a part of that |
| die Erziehungsfrage, -n | question regarding child rearing |
| der Flirt, -s | flirt |
| die Meinungsumfrage, -n | opinion survey |
| unordentlich | disorderly |
| die Unzuverlässigkeit, -en | undependability |

## Seite 74 — page 74

| aktiv | active |
| der Beamte, -n | civil servant |
| dreifach | three-time |
| das Finanzamt, ¨er | governmental revenue office |
| der Jugendtraum, ¨e | dream from one's youth |
| die Krise, -n | crisis |
| der Kulturverein, -e | culture club |
| der Lebensabschnitt, -e | excerpt from one's life |

| | |
|---|---|
| die Pension, -en (in Pension sein) | here: retirement, to be in retirement |
| *die Schauspielschule, -n* | *acting school* |
| Schuss: in Schuss kommen | shot: to hit one's stride |
| der Steckbrief, -e | here: summary of pertinent personal information |
| stehen bleiben, er ist stehen geblieben | to remain standing; to be left standing (alone) |
| *still·stehen, er hat stillgestanden* | *to stand still, come to a halt* |
| wahr werden, es wird wahr, es ist wahr geworden | to come true |

## Seite 75        page 75

| | |
|---|---|
| *das Kompositum, Komposita* | *composite* |
| *die Satzverbindung, -en* | *combining clauses/sentences* |
| unregelmäßig | irregular |

## Seite 76        page 76

| | |
|---|---|
| *das Abschiedsgedicht, -e* | *farewell poem* |
| *das Abschiedswort, -e* | *word of farewell* |
| *Ade* | *bye (from "adieu")* |
| *Auf Wiederluege* | *good-bye (in Switzerland)* |
| *das Begrüßungswort, -e* | *word of greeting* |
| *die Doppelseite, -n* | *double page* |
| *das Karaoke (Sg)* | *karaoke* |
| *die Liedstrophe, -n* | *song strophe* |
| *die Melodie, -n* | *melody* |
| nicht wahr | right? isn't that so? |
| *Salü* | *bye (from "salut")* |
| schaffen | to do it, achieve one's objective |
| *Schritt für Schritt* | *step-by-step* |
| *Tschö* | *bye (from "Tschüs")* |
| *untrennbar* | *inseparable* |
| *zu Ende gehen* | *to come to an end* |
| zusammen·gehören | to belong together |

## Seite 77        page 77

| | |
|---|---|
| *Adieu* | *adieu, farewell* |
| *auseinander gehen, sie sind auseinander gegangen* | *to go separate ways, to disband* |
| *ein·kehren* | *to come in for something to eat* |
| *das Fräulein, –* | *miss* |
| *Lebwohl* | *farewell* |
| *nachdenklich* | *pensive* |
| *reizend* | *alluring, attractive* |
| *scheiden, er ist geschieden* | *to divorce, he is divorced* |
| *das Vergnügen, –* | *pleasure* |
| *das Volkslied, -er* | *folk song* |

## Fragebogen        Questionnaire

### Seite 78        page 78

| | |
|---|---|
| *aus·werten* | *to evaluate, interpret* |
| *die Auswertung, -en* | *evaluation, interpretation* |
| der Gegensatz, ¨e | opposite |
| *die Leserumfrage, -n* | *reader survey* |
| *der Reiseprospekt, -e* | *travel brochure* |
| *der Sicherheitshinweis, -e* | *safety instruction* |
| die Stadtmitte (Sg) | city center |
| die Verkehrsmeldung, -en | traffic announcement |

### Seite 79        page 79

| | |
|---|---|
| *die Daten (Pl)* | *data* |
| *das Internetforum, -foren* | *internet or online forum* |
| *der Kommentar, -e* | *commentary* |
| *der Lieblingsgegenstand, ¨e* | favorite object |
| *nach·erzählen* | *to retell* |
| *die Ortsangabe, -n* | *location (designation of location)* |
| weiter·leben | to continue living |

## Arbeitsbuch        Workbook

### Seite 144        page 144

| | |
|---|---|
| *der Campingurlaub, -e* | *camping vacation* |
| die Jugend (Sg) | youth (period of life) |
| das Kinderbuch, ¨er | children's book |
| mit·arbeiten | to work together, collaborate |

### Seite 145        page 145

| | |
|---|---|
| *ab·warten* | *to wait (for something)* |
| *der Pickel, –* | *pimple* |
| *das Schuljahr, -e* | *school year* |
| *der Schultag, -e* | *school day* |
| *unattraktiv* | *unattractive* |
| die Wahrheit, -en | truth |

### Seite 146        page 146

| | |
|---|---|
| erziehen, er hat erzogen | to educate, raise |
| die Hälfte, -n | half |
| *die Märchenwelt (Sg)* | *fairy-tale world* |

### Seite 147        page 147

| | |
|---|---|
| *die Partnerschaft, -en* | *partnership* |
| *der Satzanfang, ¨e* | *beginning of a sentence or phrase* |
| *der Traummann, ¨er* | *dream man* |

# Forms and Structures

## 1 Review: Perfect tense *(Wiederholung: Perfekt)*

examples

*Ich **habe** nicht **gewusst**, dass Babys so klein sind.*    I didn't know that babies are so small.

*Guck mal, deine Urgroßtante **ist gekommen**.*    Look! Your great-great-aunt came.

*Ich **habe** auf einer Baustelle **gespielt** und **bin** in ein Loch **gefallen**.*    I was playing on a construction site and fell in a hole.

In *Schritte international 1*, Chapter 7 you learned that, when talking about the past, German speakers generally use the *Perfekt*. This tense is overwhelmingly used in spoken German. The *Perfekt* requires an auxiliary, or helping verb and the past participle of the principal verb.

### a auxiliary verbs:

90% of German verbs form the *Perfekt* with *haben* as the auxiliary verb:
*habe gewusst*
*habe gespielt*

Verbs indicating a change of position or condition use *sein* as their auxiliary verb:
*ist gekommen*
*bin gefallen*

A handful of other verbs form the *Perfekt* with *sein*:
| | |
|---|---|
| *sein:* | *Er ist früher selbstständig gewesen.* |
| *bleiben:* | *Wir sind das ganze Wochenende zu Hause geblieben.* |
| *passieren:* | *Was ist denn passiert?* |

### b past participles:

Past participles are usually formed with the prefix *ge-* and a suffix; in the case of weak verbs, the suffix is *-t*:
*ge-spiel-t*

Strong and irregular verbs' participles end in *-en*:
*ge-komm-en*

and some change their stem vowel:
*ge-blie-ben*

examples

***Hast** du **vergessen**, dass wir heute Abend Konzert haben?*
*Kurt **hat** uns für morgen **eingeladen**, ich **habe** heute mit ihm **telefoniert**.*

Participles of verbs with separable prefixes place the syllable *ge-* between the prefix and the verb stem.
*ein-ge-laden*

Verbs with inseparable prefixes have no *ge-* syllable:
*vergessen*

nor do verbs ending in *-ieren*.
*telefoniert*

(See *Schritte international 3*, Chapter 1).

## 2    Review: *Präteritum (Wiederholung: Präteritum)*

examples    *Meine Eltern **hatten** einen Lebensmittelladen.*    My parents had a grocery.

*Meine Oma **war** immer fröhlich.*    My grandma was always cheerful.

*Meine Schwester und ich **mussten** mithelfen.*    My sister and I had to help out.

With the verbs *sein, haben* and the modal verbs, the *Präteritum* form of each verb is preferred when speaking about the past. (See *Schritte international 2*, Chapter 8 and *Schritte international 3*, Chapter 6.)

examples    *Mit 18 Jahren **machte** ich mein Abitur, danach **studierte** ich Medizin. Nach dem Studium **ging** ich für ein Jahr ins Ausland.*    At 18 I did my Abitur, after that I studied medicine. After my studies I went abroad for a year.

With other verbs, the *Präteritum* is preferred in written texts.

The *Präteritum* of weak verbs is characterized by the syllable *-te-*:
mach-te                studier-te

Strong and irregular verbs often change their stem vowels, and there is no ending on the 1st and 3rd person singular forms:
ich ging                er/es/sie ging

## 3    Review: *Konjunktiv II  (Wiederholung: Konjunktiv II)*

examples    *Maria **hätte** gern etwas Ruhe.*    Maria would like to have some peace and quiet.

*Larissa **würde** das Baby gern Belinda **nennen**.*    Larissa would really like to name the baby Belinda.

*Ich **möchte** bitte einen Kaffee.*    I'd like a coffee, please.

To state a request politely and with less directness than a command, the constructions *hätte gern, würde gern* or *möchte* are often used. Such verb forms are called *Konjunktiv II*.
Most verbs form the *Konjunktiv II* using the auxiliary verb *würd-* and the infinitive of the principal verb (*würde ... nennen*).
Some verbs that are used frequently in the *Konjunktiv* (sein, haben, modal verbs) usually are expressed using their own forms instead of the *würde*-construction (*wäre, hätte, möchte, etc.*).

examples    *Wir **könnten** mal wieder zusammen Tennis spielen.*    We could play tennis together again.

*Mit diesem Husten **sollten** Sie besser zum Arzt gehen.*    With that cough, you really should go to the doctor.

Proposals or suggestions are often expressed with the *Konjunktiv II* of the verb *können*, while advice is often expressed with the *Konjunktiv II* of the verb *sollen*.

Remember that the *Konjunktiv II* and *Präteritum* forms of *sollen* are identical. Context makes the difference clear:

examples    *Petra **sollte** mir die Zeitung mitbringen, aber sie hat es vergessen.*    Petra was supposed to bring me the newspaper, but she forgot to.

# Forms and Structures

**4**     **Review: Word building** *(Wiederholung: Wortbildung)*

**a**   adjectives

**– adjectives derived from nouns or verbs**

examples   *Wer findet das schon lustig?*     Who thinks that's funny?

*Die Deutschen sind bei Kosenamen eher einfallslos.*     Germans are rather unimaginative when it comes to nicknames/pet names.

*Die meisten sind dankbar, wenn ihr Partner sie mit ihrem richtigen Namen anspricht.*     Most people are grateful when their partner addresses them by the right name.

With the suffix *-ig*, adjectives can be derived from nouns. The resulting adjective is thus related in meaning to the noun upon which it is based:
*die Ruhe* (quiet, stillness) → *ruhig* (quiet, peaceful)
*die Lust* (now: desire, but in the past: humor ) → *lustig* (funny, humorous)

The suffix *-los* also converts nouns to adjectives. It signifies absence of something and is equivalent to *ohne*:
*der Einfall* (idea, inspiration) → *einfallslos* (uninspired, unimaginative)
*die Arbeit* (work) → *arbeitslos* (unemployed)

Adjective with the suffix *-bar* are derived from verbs. The suffix *-bar* can often be substituted with the verb *können*:
*erkennen* → *erkennbar* (recognizable, can be recognized),

but this is not always the case:
*danken* (to thank) → *dankbar* (thankful, grateful)

**– adjectives derived from other adjectives**

examples   *Sie empfinden Kosenamen als unangenehm.*     They find pet names uncomfortable.

The prefix *un-* always negates an adjective and makes it into the opposite of its root:
*angenehm* (pleasant, comfortable) → *unangenehm* (disagreeable, uncomfortable)
*freundlich* (friendly) → *unfreundlich* (unfriendly).

**b**   nouns

**– compound nouns: noun+noun**

examples   *Seit zwei Jahren spiele ich in einer Theatergruppe mit.*     I've been acting in a theater group for two years.

Long words in German are usually compounds composed of two or more individual words. The meaning of the compound is discerable by understanding the individual components:
*die Theaterguppe* → *das Theater + die Gruppe*
*der Arbeitskollege* → *die Arbeit + der Kollege*

Remember that the gender of a compound noun is always determined by the gender of the final component.

das Theater + **die** Gruppe       → **die** Theatergruppe
die Arbeit + **der** Kollege        → **der** Arbeitskollege

### – nouns derived from nouns

examples    *Berichten Sie über Ihren Partner/Ihre Partnerin.*        Talk about your partner.

*Kosewörter wie „Häschen" sind sehr populär.*        Pet names such as "bunny" are very popular.

In *Schritte international 2*, Chapter 8, you learned that the suffix *-in* creates the feminine of any number of personal nouns:
*der Partner → die Partnerin*
*der Freund → die Freundin.*

The syllable *-chen* is used to form a diminutive. Nouns with this suffix (as with the diminutive suffix *-lein*) are always neuter:
*der Hase → das Häschen*
*der Tisch → das Tischchen.*

The syllable *-chen* often causes the vowels *a, o* and *u* to umlaut in the noun stem (as does *-lein*).

### – nouns derived from verbs

examples    *Wir haben zehn Familien befragt.*        We surveyed ten families.
*Die Befragung hat gezeigt …*        The survey showed …

*Du solltest nicht so viel rauchen,*        You shouldn't smoke so much.
*Raucher leben gefährlich.*        Smokers live dangerously.

Nouns ending in *-ung* are derived from verbs and are always feminine:
*befragen → die Befragung.*

There are some nouns for which there is no longer a clear path to the verb of their origin, such as:
*die Zeitung.*

The suffix *-er* transforms action verbs into nouns designating the person performing the action. This suffix always makes the noun masculine, and the corresponding pronoun is *er*. (To denote that the doer is a female, the suffix *-in* is then also added.)
*rauchen → der Raucher*
*lehren → der Lehrer*

**5**  **Review: combining clauses** *(Wiederholung: Satzverbindungen)*

**a**  **Main clause + subordinate clause:** *wenn, weil, das*

examples | | |
|---|---|
| *Du wirst es ja sehen, **wenn** du mich besuchst.* | You'll see if/when you visit me. |
| *Sie haben gestritten, **weil** sie sich nicht einigen konnten.* | They argued because they could not agree. |
| *Ich freue mich, **dass** du mich besuchst.* | I'm happy that you're visiting me! |

The conjunctions *wenn*, *weil* and *dass* introduce subordinate clauses, phrases that depend on another clause to complete their meaning. Remember that in German, the clauses are always separated by a comma, and the subordinate clause has its conjugated verb in final position!

*Wenn* expresses both a temporal relationship (when) and a conditional relationship (if).
*Weil* indicates a causal relationship.
Statements with *dass* usually perform a complementary function:
*Ich freue mich über deinen Besuch.*
        *…, dass du mich besuchst.*

With *dass*, it is important to remember that the "that" designated by *dass* is not the same as the demonstrative pronoun *das*, which in English is also "that":
*Das ist nicht gut.*                  That's not good.
*Ich weiß, dass es etwas Besseres gibt.*   I know that there is something better.

**b**  **Main clause + main clause:** *aber, denn, deshalb, trotzdem*

examples | | |
|---|---|
| *Ich wollte zum Theater, **aber** meine Mutter konnte die Schaupielschule nicht bezahlen.* | I wanted to go into theater, but my mother couldn't afford acting school. |
| *Wir sind glücklich, **denn** wir lieben uns.* | We're happy because we love each other. |

The conjunctions *aber* and *denn* join two main clauses, so word order does not change (the conjugated verb in both clauses remains in second position). *Aber* expresses contradition, *denn* expresses causality.

examples | | |
|---|---|
| *Du hast fast nie Zeit für mich, **deshalb** bin ich sauer.* | You almost never have time for me, therefore, I'm ticked off. |
| *Ich räume dauernd auf, **trotzdem** ist es hier nie ordentlich.* | I'm constantly straightening up, but in spite of that it's never neat here. |

*Trotzdem* and *deshalb* also express contradiction and causality (respectively), and they join main clauses. But in constrast to *aber* and *denn*, *deshalb* and *trotzdem* function like adverbs within the larger sentence; the verb is in second position, and *deshalb* or *trotzdem* comes either directly before or after the verb, with the subject in the other position around it (*ich bin deshalb sauer, es ist trotzdem hier nie ordentlich*).

**6**  **Translate into English.**

**a**  *Als ich Kind war, hat mir meine Mutter oft* .................................................

*vorgelesen. Ich habe das dann mit meinen* .................................................

*Kindern auch gemacht.* .................................................

*– Bei uns zu Hause haben wir viel gesungen.* .................................................

**b**  *Wir könnten mal wieder ins Theater gehen,* .................................................

*oder möchtest du lieber einen Film sehen?* .................................................

*– Am liebsten würde ich mal in die Oper* .................................................

*gehen, da war ich noch nie.* .................................................

**c**  *Das Buch hat mir gut gefallen, es ist sehr* .................................................

*lustig.* .................................................

*– Ach ja? Mir hat es überhaupt nicht* .................................................

*gefallen. Ich finde die Geschichte ziemlich* .................................................

*einfallslos.* .................................................

**7**  **Translate into English.**

**a**  *Tanja hat sich schon zweimal scheiden lassen,* .................................................

*trotzdem will sie wieder heiraten.* .................................................

*– Hast du ihren neuen Freund denn* .................................................

*schon kennengelernt?* .................................................

**b**  *Hm, die Schokolade schmeckt aber lecker.* .................................................

*Darf ich noch ein Stückchen haben?* 

*– Ja natürlich. Hier, nimm!* .................................................

**c**  *Ich finde es gut, wenn man mit seinem* .................................................

*Partner über alles reden kann.* .................................................

*– Ich auch, aber es ist es auch wichtig,* .................................................

*dass man richtig zuhört.*

**8**   **Translate into German.**

**a**   What happened?

..............................................................

– I fixed my bike and hurt myself

..............................................................

doing it.

................................*dabei*...............................

Should we go to the doctor?

..............................................................

**b**   As a child, I always wanted to be a

..............................................................

musician, and then I became a German

*dann*.........................................................

teacher.

..............................................................

– Couldn't you be both?

................................*beides*...............................

**c**   You should take the subway, there's a

..............................................................

lot of traffic today.

..........................*ist*..........*Verkehr.*............

– You're right, but I'd rather go by car,

..............................................................

it's more comfortable.

..............................................................

**9**   **Translate into German.**

**a**   I've got to save. I'd like to buy

..............................................................

a little house on the beach.

..............................................................

– Where do you want to buy one?

..............................................................

**b**   This evening, there's a concert in the

..............................................................

Conservatory. It's free, starts at 7:30.

*Konservatorium*...................................................

– Oh, I'd like to go to that. Should we

..............................................................

meet at the entrance at seven?

..............................................................

**c**   How's the weather on the coast right now?

..............................................................

– It's very windy and cold, unpleasant

..............................................................

weather.

..............................................................

Oh well, it can't always be sunny.

..............................................................

## Listening and Pronunciation

The <ch> in the diminutive suffix *-chen* is pronounced as an *ich-Laut* (such as *ich* and *rechts*).

*Schwesterchen*
*Bärchen*
*Häuschen*

## Familiarity and Understanding

### Of pregnant oysters and hollow teeth

German has a very appropriate name for the common vernacular of a language: *Volksmund*, literally, "the people's mouth". And every culture has its own peculiar names for different buildings, neighborhoods and even entire cities. Still, few regions can match Berlin for the sheer humor and inventiveness of some of their nicknames. The *Haus der Kulturen der Welt*, for example, the House of World Cultures with its rounded and bulging form, is known among Berliners as *die Schwangere Auster* or "the pregnant oyster". It has also been called *Jimmy Carters Lächeln* (Jimmy Carter's smile). Berlin's most famous church, the *Kaiser-Wilhelm-Gedächtniskirche* (Kaiser Wilhelm Memorial Church), still standing as it has since being bombed in World War II as a reminder of the War's devastation, is missing a large chunk of its steeple point and has earned the nickname *Hohler Zahn* (hollow tooth). It has also gone by the name of *Lippenstift und Puderdose* (lipstick and powder compact) which reflects the totality of the tower and the round chapel behind it. The new Chancellery near the Reichstag has been dubbed *die Waschmaschine*, the washing machine, as a large opening at one end makes the building resemble a front-loading washer. The television tower in downtown Berlin is known as *der weiße Spargel* (the white asparagus).

The Berlin neighborhood with the highest Turkish population is known as *Klein-Istanbul*; Frankfurt is nicknamed *Mainhattan*, playing upon its location on the Main river, and it is also known by the moniker of *Bankfurt*, playing upon its role as the hometown of most large German banks as well as the European Central Bank.
Cars get fun names, too: beyond the *Käfer*, the Volkswagen Beetle of old, *Trabi* is the nickname of the East German *Trabant*.

Germans themselves have been given nicknames, and not particularly flattering ones: alongside the English *Krauts*, Luxemburgers call them *Preis* (Prussians) and the Austrians use *Piefke* (usually pejorative).

### One square meter for an hour – another living model

Looking for a room? Can't afford one?

Students at the Technical University of Darmstadt (west of Frankfurt) had this problem in 1992 and came up with a novel initiative that continues not just in several German cities but in other countries as well. Many senior citizens need help around the house or they need someone to spend time with, while many university students need a place to live but don't have the income to afford much. Both attend a town hall meeting where they meet and see who matches to whom, and then the student moves into the home of their senior citizen "match". The baseline calculation of service in exchange for housing is one hour per square meter of living area. Hence, a student living in a 15 m² room would provide 15 hours of service per month plus a share of the common utilities. Students do not provide health care or personal assistance; tasks they can be asked to perform include work in the house or  yard, or running errands. The mutual benefits to seniors and students have created a following for the program, known as *Wohnen für Hilfe* in Germany and as Homesharing in the United States. The arrangement not only allows the seniors to stay in their own homes and for students to live affordably, but it also gives both generations the chance to interact and benefit from each others' energy and experience.

Ten cities participate in *Wohnen für Hilfe*; to find the proper contact for more information in each city, see www.wohnenfuerhilfe.info.

### "I want to remain an eternal enigma, to myself and to the world ..." – the legacy of a mythical king, the symbol of German tourism

When Donald Trump overspends on the construction of his hotels, he may draw public scorn and criticism, and he may even need to file for bankruptcy protection, but no one would think to unseat him as the head of his company on grounds of mental incapacity. Not all property developers have fared as well as Trump, however, and we introduced you to one such example in Chapter 4 of *Schritte international* Glossary XXL Vol. 1. Ludwig II von Bayern, known as *der Märchenkönig* (the Fairy Tale King) is also known as "Mad King Ludwig" for the controversy surrounding his deposition.

Ludwig ascended to his throne at the age of 18, and from the outset showed little interest in matters of state or in public appearances. Ludwig preferred walking through the countryside and chatting with farmers or immersing himself in the music of Richard Wagner (he attended performances of Wagner's operas, but not public ones). His common touch, combined with his taste for extravagant housing, endeared him to his subjects, but caused endless consternation for his advisors and ministers. Their feeling was that a king should primarily be concerned with his rule, not building castles in the mountains.

Clearly, this was a sentiment the King did not share. In addition to Neuschwanstein, near to his family's castle Hohenschwangau in Allgäu, Ludwig also commissioned the construction of two other castles and a royal apartment in the *Residenz* Palace in Munich.

Ludwig's plan for what became known after his death as Neuschwanstein was to recreate an ancient castle whose ruins were located nearby, following the model of a knight's castle, and dedicated to the genius of Richard Wagner. Most of the castle's interior is dedicated to Wagner's operas, with frescoes in several rooms representing scenes from them. Particular emphasis is placed on the operas based on Nordic and Germanic legends, but scenes from *Die Meistersänger von Nürnberg* are present as well. The King's wooden-paneled bedroom alone took 14 carpenters 4 years to finish. Such detailed craftsmanship does not come cheap. Ludwig never spent a penny of state funds on his castles, but he did go personally into deep debt and borrowed extensively from outside sources, including the Prussian government, to finance his creative endeavors. His loans from Prussia especially forced him into political alliances he would otherwise never have entered, further consternating his ministers. When the German Reich was declared, Ludwig was required to submit to the Kaiser's authority, partly due to his monetary indebtedness to Prussia, the Kaiser's kingdom. He was so frustrated by this turn of events that he refused to attend the Kaiser's coronation.

Ludwig was always eccentric, but his continued withdrawal from public life led his ministers to consult with four psychiatrists who declared Ludwig to be suffering from paranoia and thus mentally unfit to rule, though none of them had even met Ludwig, let alone examined him. At 4 a.m. on June 12, 1886, Ludwig II was deposed and succeeded by his uncle Luitpold. Ludwig was living in Neuschwanstein at the time, which by then had been under construction for 17 years. He was transported to Castle Berg on the shore of Lake Starnberg, accompanied by one of the four psychiatrists who had declared him insane.

Three days later, Ludwig and the doctor were both found drowned in shallow water in Lake Starnberg. His death was ruled a suicide, though no real evidence either of suicide or homicide was ever found. The circumstances of his death have only served to make him more enigmatic, something he no doubt would have enjoyed.

Just weeks later on August 1, 1886, and entirely against the stated wishes of the late King, Neuschwanstein opened its doors to the public. Though it had become Ludwig's financial ruin and a thorn in the side of Bavaria, which had been a free country until Ludwig's indebtedness subjected it to Prussia, it has since been a financial boon to the region, even as its upkeep has cost the State of Bavaria over 14 million Euros since 1990.

Neuschwanstein has drawn an endless stream of visitors for over a century, averaging 6,000 per day in the summer, and 1.3 million per year. The attraction it holds is ironic, considering that Ludwig intended the castle to serve as a retreat away from the masses. It now serves as an icon of Germany, the model for Sleeping Beauty's castle in the Disney film (and the brand image for Disney itself), and in 2007 it was a finalist in a vote on the New Seven Wonders of the World. (It was not chosen, and now is advertised as the Eighth Wonder.)

### Laughing at his own shadow: Wilhelm Busch – the father of the comic strip

Before there was Curious George, there was Fipps the Monkey; before there was Dennis the Menace, there were Max and Moritz.

Just as every American child knows Dennis the Menace, every German child knows Max and Moritz, the most famous of Wilhelm Busch's characters. The original naughty boys, whose pranks hearken back to Till Eulenspiegel but are much more damaging, first appeared in publication in 1865, and have been translated about three hundred times (it was the first foreign children's book to be published in Japan). Unlike Dennis, however, after seven nasty pranks, the terrible twosome in Busch's work meet a macabre fate, as do the protagonists of almost all Busch's works.

Originally sent to study engineering, Wilhelm Busch (1832–1908) soon left the Polytechnicum and began to study painting. He soon showed talent not only for visual arts (after his death, over 1100 small oils were found) but also for pithy, often onomotopaetic couplets. His illustrated stories were accompanied by rhyming texts, and many of the couplets contained therein have become among the most quoted items in the German language. Indeed, only Goethe and Schiller are quoted more in German than Busch.

The grotesque features and brutal ends of many of Busch's characters relate directly to his affinity for the rather pessimistic philosophy of Arthur Schopenhauer. His stories take a humorous but very critical view of everyday life. Nothing escaped Busch's gaze, and he used his verbal and artistic talents to exaggerate and highlight the smug satisfaction of most people's daily life.

Today, Wilhelm Busch is considered to be the father of the modern comic strip and of animated film. His ability to combine language and image to create a sense of activity in still cartoons prefigured 20th century animation, and his changing perspectives (which lent themselves to often garish exaggeration) are the forerunner of the same technique in comic books and novels. But in spite of such virtuosity, what he will always be best known for are the seven pranks of two bad boys who mercilessly plagued their neighbors, and who met an equally merciless end.

## Historical Fragments

### Romans, Germans and the beginnings of Germany history

Magna Germania, the territory between the Rhine and Elbe rivers north of the Danube river was a de facto province of the Roman Empire under Caesar Augustus for a relatively short time. His stepsons

Germanicus and Tiberius had conquered this territory and forged alliances with a number of Germanic princes. Quinctilius Varus, the Governor of this period, was a man with little battle experience; Arminius, the son of a German prince who had trained with the Roman army, took advantage of the Governor's weakness and won back territory in alliance with other Germanic tribes. In the Battle of the Teutoburg Forest (near the modern-day city of Osnabrück) in the year 9 A.D., Arminius and his forces defeated and annihilated Quinctilius' three legions. This military disaster (immortalized in Heinrich von Kleist's drama *die Hermannsschlacht*) ended Caesar Augustus' ambitions for expanding the Empire, and it left the region free of Romanization.

The Romans in turn sought to fortify their position on the left bank of the Rhine. Recent archaeological excavations have found evidence of further failed attempts to reconquer Germania. But the Romans did not only pursue military goals; emerging cities such as Cologne, Regensburg and Augsburg brought cultural and commercial innovations into Germania that had a profound effect on the lives of the Germanic people, for example in agriculture.

Germania was not populated or ruled by a single Germanic tribe; Saxons, Alemanni, Goths, Franks and Frisians all claimed their own territories while intersecting and integrating with other tribes.

Around 375, the Huns invaded German territory, drawing the Germanic tribes into wars. As the tribes fled to the southeast, the borders on the west (along the Rhine) and the south (the Limes Germanicus) were closed and fortified. Subsequent Hun encroachments in the 5th century prompted some to flee, ushering in what Germans now refer to as *die Völkerwanderung* (Period of Great Migration) leading to the fall of the Western Roman Empire and the rise of the Franks (476), which we examined in the previous chapter of this volume. These invasions ended with the Lombard conquest of northern Italy (568).

The migrations created German empires in the west and south: the Suebi in western Spain, the Visigoths in central Spain (Toledo, 507), the Burgundian settlement at Savoy (443), the rule of the Franks in Gaul (after 486), that of the Ostrogoths in Italy (until 552) and the Vandals in southern Spain and northern Africa (until 534). The Anglo-Saxons conquered Britain after Roman troops withdrew to Gaul in 407.

Following a bloody conquest, Germanic tribes began to slowly mix with the Roman population. Throughout their domain, the Germanic tribes accepted Roman forms of administration and jurisprudence. But most influential factor upon the Germans was the gradual conversion to Christianity, which became the state religion of the Roman Empire in 391.

The Franks' victories over other Germanic tribes (the Burgundians, the Alemanni, and the Visigoths) allowed them to extend their reign across a territory that extended from the Ebro to the Elbe.

In 732, Charles Martel, grandfather of Charlemagne, halted a Muslim advance from Spain at Tours (also known as Poitiers). His son Pépin the Short supported the Pope against the Lombards and defeated them, as we saw in the previous chapter. The Pope rewarded him with the conquered territory and thus founded the Papal States (754). In turn, Pépin's son Charlemagne was crowned Emperor by the Pope, laying the foundation for the Holy Roman Empire, placing Italy and the Pope under the protection of a German sovereign. German rule thus led Western Christianity until the beginning of the 13th century.

## Self-Evaluation

**Stages of Life**

### When listening, I can understand (Hören)

– someone's childhood memories: *„Wir durften immer im Stall mithelfen."*
– interviews on everyday subjects: *Interview mit einem Ehepaar*
– a song about one stage in life: *(Udo Jürgens)*

### In written texts, I can understand (Lesen)

– statistics and opinion polls, and what their results mean: *Worüber streiten Paare am häufigsten?*
– a letter about an important family event: *„Liebe Karin, das Baby ist da. Es ist so ein süßes Mädchen!"*
– a text on someone's life: *„Mit 16 hast du natürlich Träume ..."*
– letters to a medical column in a magazine: *„Ich weiß nicht mehr, was ich machen soll."*

### I can produce the following oral structures (Sprechen)

– describing my childhood: *„Ich bin auf dem Land aufgewachsen, in einem kleinen Dorf, ..."*
– my future plans: *„... mit 46 möchte ich Erfolg im Beruf haben. Und ich hoffe, dass meine Eltern noch fit sind ..."*
– give advice or suggestions regarding certain problems that young people have: *„... du solltest mit Freunden ausgehen ..."*

### I can produce the following written texts (Schreiben)

– a response to a letter sent to an advice columnist: *„... du könntest im neuen Schuljahr Nachhilfe nehmen."*
– I short love story: *„Eduard wollte im April mit dem Zug nach Glasgow fahren. Deshalb ..."*

# Vocabulary

| Wiederholungs-stationen | Review Stations |
| --- | --- |

## Seite 150 — page 150

| der Autoreifen, – | automobile tire |
| --- | --- |
| das Schokoladeneis (Sg) | chocolate ice cream |
| der Schwimmer, – | swimmer |
| das Spielauto, -s | toy car |

## Seite 151 — page 151

| der Bauernschrank, ⸚e | cabinet or armoire in a farmhouse style |
| --- | --- |
| der Eimer, – | bucket, pail |
| das Wochenendangebot, -e | weekend price (special offer) |

## Seite 152 — page 152

| die Mannschaft, -en | team |
| --- | --- |

## Seite 153 — page 153

| der Hotelparkplatz, ⸚e | hotel parking lot |
| --- | --- |
| der Kurzurlaub, -e | short vacation |

## Seite 154 — page 154

| die Kartoffelsuppe, -n | potato soup |
| --- | --- |
| das Passbild, -er | ID photo |
| das Stadtfest, -e | city festival |

## Seite 155 — page 155

| der Schulfreund, -e | school friend |
| --- | --- |

## Seite 156 — page 156

| die Stehlampe, -n | floor lamp |
| --- | --- |

| Prüfungstraining | Examination training |
| --- | --- |

## Seite 158 — page 158

| das Inhaltsverzeichnis, -se | table of contents |
| --- | --- |
| kontrollieren | to check |
| die Problemlösung, -en | solution to the/a problem |

| die Radioinformation, -en | radio information |
| --- | --- |
| der Straßenname, -n | street name |

## Seite 159 — page 159

| die Telefon-Notiz, -en | telephone message note |
| --- | --- |

## Seite 160 — page 160

| der Club, -s | club |
| --- | --- |
| die Filmmusik, -en | music from the/a film |
| gehen um (Worum geht es?) | to be about/have to do with (What's it about?) |
| der Hinweis, -e | indication, instruction, tip |
| öffentlich | public |
| der Radiohörer, – | radio listener |
| der Verkehrsinformation, -en | traffic information |

## Seite 161 — page 161

| das Chefbüro, -s | boss' office |
| --- | --- |
| der Computerraum, ⸚e | computer room |
| das Kästchen, – | small box |
| das Konferenzzimmer, – | conference room |
| der Monatsname, -n | name of the month |
| die Prüfungsvorbereitung, -en | examination preparation |
| die Teeküche, -n | tea kitchen (small kitchen for drink and snack preparation) |

## Seite 162 — page 162

| die Antiquität, -en | antique |
| --- | --- |
| das Ballett (Sg) | ballet |
| bestimmt | here: certain |
| die Bevölkerung (Sg) | population |
| der Freizeitsport (Sg) | leisure sports |
| die Informationstafel, -n | information panel |
| das Jugendgästehaus, ⸚er | guest house for young people |
| das Kulturzentrum, -zentren | cultural center |
| die Mitwohnzentrale, -n | roommate placement agency |
| das Musical, -s | musical |
| die Reisevorbereitung, -en | trip reservation |
| die Reisezeit, -en | here: tourist season |
| die Rubrik, -en | rubric |
| sehenswert | worth seeing |
| die Teestube, -n | tea room |
| die Wellness, – | wellness |

## Seite 163 — page 163

| die Abgabe, -n | delivery, submission |
| --- | --- |
| ab·schneiden, er hat abgeschnitten | here: to score |
| ab·stürzen | to crash |

# Vocabulary

| | |
|---|---|
| beruhigen | to calm |
| *die Doktorarbeit, -en* | *doctoral dissertation* |
| *empirisch* | *empirical* |
| *erwachsen* | *adult* |
| *die Gaststudentin, -nen* | *visiting student* |
| die Grundschullehrerin, -nen | elementary school teacher |
| die Hauptschullehrerin, -nen | secondary school teacher |
| lohnen (sich) | to be worth it |
| *der Mitstudent, -en* | *fellow student* |
| die Praxis (Sg) | practice |
| *probeweise* | *on a test basis* |
| *die Promotion, -en* | *awarding of a doctoral degree* |
| *promovieren* | *to earn a doctoral degree* |
| retten | to save |
| stolz | proud |
| *das Studentenleben, –* | *student life* |
| *stürzen (sich)* | here: to hurl oneself |
| *verzweifelt* | *desparate* |
| der Vorteil, -e | advantage |

## Seite 164 — page 164

| | |
|---|---|
| *die Au-pair-Vermittlung, -en* | *au pair agency* |
| *der Babysitter, –* | *babysitter* |
| *die Bestimmung, -en* | *regulation* |
| die Bundeshauptstadt (Sg) | Federal capital (city) |
| *engagiert* | *committed, dedicated* |
| *englischsprachig* | *English-speaking* |
| *das Entertainment (Sg)* | *entertainment* |
| *entsprechend* | *corresponding* |
| *die Gastronomie (Sg)* | *gastronomy* |
| *die Jobvermittlung, -en* | *work placement agency* |
| *die Kinderbetreuung (Sg)* | *child care* |
| *der Nachhilfelehrer, –* | *tutor* |
| *die Pauschalreise, -n* | *package trip* |
| *der Reiseveranstalter, –* | *trip organizer* |
| *die Rundreise, -n* | *tour* |
| *die Semesterferien (Pl)* | *semester break* |
| *die Sommersaison, -s* | *summer season* |
| spannend | tense, exciting |
| der Sportlehrer, – | sports teacher |
| *tageweise* | *day-to-day* |
| *der Tiersitter, –* | *petsitter* |
| vormittags | mornings |

## Seite 165 — page 165

| | |
|---|---|
| *die Anschrift, -en* | *(mailing) address* |
| *der Au-pair-Vertrag, ⸚e* | *au-pair contract* |
| *begeistern* | *to excite, thrill* |
| *die Behinderteneinrichtung, -en* | *facility for the disabled* |
| beraten, du berätst, er berät, er hat beraten | to advise, counsel |
| *bewährt* | *here: established, proven* |
| *der Cluburlaub, -e* | *club vacation* |

| | |
|---|---|
| *diverse* | *various* |
| *die Einsatzmöglichkeit, -en* | *placement possibility* |
| *der Frühbucher, –* | *person who books/reserves early* |
| *die Institution, -en* | *institution* |
| *jederzeit* | *at any time* |
| *das Kinderzentrum, -zentren* | *children's center* |
| *medizinisch* | *medical* |
| *die Mitarbeit (Sg)* | *collaboration* |
| *die Nachbarschaftshilfe (Sg)* | *neighborhood assistance* |
| *der Nationalpark, -s* | *national park* |
| *das Online-Forum, -Foren* | *online forum* |
| *der Reisespezialist, -en* | *travel specialist* |
| *die Schönheit, -en* | *beauty* |
| *der Seniorentreff, -s* | *seniors' get-together* |
| *sozialpädagogisch* | *sociopedagogical* |
| *das Taschengeld (Sg)* | *pocket money* |
| *tauchen* | *to dive* |
| *unbezahlt* | *unpaid* |
| *der Verband, ⸚e* | *union, alliance, association* |
| *vermitteln* | *here: to arrange for* |
| *die Visabestimmung, -en* | *visa regulation* |
| *Wasserski (Sg)* | *water skiing* |
| *Windsurfen (Sg)* | *wind surfing* |
| zahlreich | numerous |

## Seite 166 — page 166

| | |
|---|---|
| *der Anfangszeitpunkt, -e* | *beginning point in time* |
| *befreundet* | *befriended, friends* |
| *der Berufswunsch, ⸚e* | *desired profession* |
| *der Berufszweig, -e* | *branch of a profession* |
| *der Bewerber, –* | *applicant* |
| *die Elektrotechnik (Sg)* | *electrical engineering* |
| *frühestens* | *at the earliest* |
| *die Nationalität, -en* | *nationality* |
| *niederländisch* | *Dutch* |
| *die Personendaten (Pl)* | *personal data* |
| *die Radio- und Fernseh-technik (Sg)* | *radio and television technology* |
| *der Schulabschluss, ⸚e* | *school degree* |
| der Studentenausweis, -e | student identification card |
| *das Studienjahr, -e* | *academic year* |
| *verfügbar* | *available* |
| *wohnhaft* | *residing* |

## Seite 168 — page 168

| | |
|---|---|
| *der Computerspezialist, -en* | *computer specialist* |
| *der Fragesatz, ⸚e* | *interrogative sentence* |
| *der Kursleiter, –* | *course leader* |
| weg·legen | to set aside, put away |

## Seite 169 — page 169

| | |
|---|---|
| *die Sporthalle, -n* | *sports center* |

## Answers to the XXL Exercises

## Chapter 8

**4   Translate into English.**
**a** It's already late. In spite of that, Lisa is still preparing food for tomorrow.
**b** Nina shouldn't spend so much time on the phone. In spite of that, she calls her girlfriends every day.
**c** We would really like to invite you and your wife for a glass of wine (our treat). – That's very nice of you, we would love to come.
**d** Laura, couldn't we play cards together again some-time? – Yeah, good idea. How would Saturday be? Can you (all) do it then?

**5   Translate into German.**
**a** Peter und Lena lieben sich sehr. Trotzdem streiten sie sich oft. / Sie streiten sich trotzdem oft.
**b** Ich bin immer sehr müde, wenn ich ins Bett gehe. Trotzdem kann ich (dann) nicht schlafen. / Ich kann (dann) trotzdem nicht schlafen. Was soll ich machen? – Ich würde mal zum Arzt gehen.
**c** Am Wochenende könnten wir mal (wieder) ins Kino gehen. Hast du Lust? – Ich würde gern (mit)gehen, aber ich habe Gäste.
**d** Wir sind nach Nizza gefahren und liegen jetzt hier am Strand. Das Wetter ist klasse. – Wie schön! Da wären wir jetzt auch gerne. Hier regnet es.

**6   Translate into German.**
**a** Was machen Sie im Urlaub, Frau Schmidt? – Ich weiß es noch nicht. Ich würde gern nach Ägypten fahren, aber mein Mann möchte lieber hier bleiben.
**b** Gehen wir zu Fuß oder fahren wir mit dem Auto? – Ich würde lieber zu Fuß gehen. Ich habe den ganzen Tag gesessen.
**c** Könntet ihr bitte das Radio ausmachen? Ich hätte gern ein bisschen Ruhe. – Magst du (denn) keine Musik?
**d** Wenn ich mit dem Studium fertig bin, würde ich gern einen Master machen. – Ich nicht, ich würde lieber gleich arbeiten.

## Chapter 9

**4   Translate into English.**
**a** The scarf is pretty, isn't it? – Hm, I don't know, this one seems prettier to me.
**b** What do you think of the travel case? – Not bad, but a suitcase is more practical.
**c** What do you think of this coffeepot? – Hm, I think it's a little too big. Wouldn't you rather buy a smaller coffeepot?
**d** Look at those shoes! – They're very expensive. Better to buy cheaper shoes.

**5   Translate into English.**
**a** I brought you something. – What? – Soccer shoes (football cleats). – Oh, they're great!
**b** What do you spend most of your money on? – I like to buy clothes, but I spend the most money on vacation.
**c** Excuse me, where can you eat inexpensively here? – The most inexpensive is at pizzeria "Verdi".
**d** Can I help you? –Yes, please. I'm looking for a dark suit with an elegant jacket.

**6   Translate into German.**
**a** Wie findest du diese Schuhe (hier)? – Sind die nicht zu leicht? – Nein, ich suche ja gerade leichte Schuhe!
**b** Oh, was ist denn das? – Das sind alte Bücher. Ich habe sie auf dem Flohmarkt gefunden.
**c** Sieh mal, da ist eine schwarze Jacke. – Ja, aber ich brauche keine schwarze Jacke, ich möchte eine braune Jacke.
**d** Kann ich Ihnen helfen? – Ja, bitte. Ich suche einen langen Rock aus einem leichten Stoff.

**7   Translate into German.**
**a** Das ist ein sehr gutes Handy. – Ja, aber mir gefällt das hier besser.
**b** Die grüne Kette gefällt mir besser als die blauen Ohrringe. – Ja, aber die Ohrringe sind billiger.
**c** Heute ist schöneres Wetter als gestern. – Ja, wir könn-ten (doch) einen kleinen Ausflug machen, meinst du nicht?
**d** Wofür geben Sie mehr Geld aus, für das Auto oder für (die) Kleidung? – Für das Auto geben wir genauso viel Geld aus wie für Kleidung.

## Chapter 10

**5 Translate into English.**
**a** They're building a big supermarket here. – Oh yeah? On this street, there are two already!
**b** What's with the new camera? – It's just being tested. If everything is OK, they'll put it on the market next month.
**c** There's been a lot of discussion lately on the topic of "women's speech – men's speech". – True, and what's your opinion/take?
**d** The windows in our office are already completely filthy. – Aren't they ever cleaned? / Don't they ever get cleaned?

**6 Translate into English.**
**a** I'm looking for a nice book for my colleague. – What kinds of books does he like to read?
**b** I'd like to buy a new bike. – And what kind of bike would you like? A mountain bike.

# Answers to the XXL Exercises

c If you buy 2 DVDs, you get the 3rd one free. –
Outstanding, then I'll take four.
d The old cuckoo clock is keeping very bad time. We
have to take it to be fixed. – I can take it tomorrow.

**7   Translate into German.**
a Wie macht man Apfelstrudel? – Ich weiß (es) nicht.
Wir könnten das Rezept doch im Internet suchen.
b Hier wird viel gearbeitet, aber man verdient auch viel.
Interessiert Sie die Stelle? – Ich bin nicht sicher.
c Wie gefällt dir der neue Bildschirm? – Sehr gut, viel
besser als der alte.
d Ich glaube, ich kaufe den roten Pullover mit den weißen Streifen.– Den würde ich nicht kaufen. Der gelbe
gefällt mir besser.

**8 Translate into German.**
a Was für Fragen kommen denn in dem Test? – Keine
über Grammatik.
b Welches Handy gefällt dir besser, das schwarze oder
das blaue? – Das blaue. Willst du auch eine Handytasche
dafür?
c In dieses Geschäft komme ich nicht wieder. Die
Verkäuferin ist sehr unsympathisch. – Ja, sie ist unhöflich
und macht ihre Arbeit lustlos.
d Was für Pläne habt ihr fürs Wochenende? – Ich weiß
es noch nicht. Vielleicht fahren wir in die Berge.

## Chapter 11

**5   Translate into English.**
a Would you all like fresh rolls? I just came from shop-
ping. – No thank you, we were just at the bakery and
brought some ourselves.
b Hi Monika, it's Manfred. I'm just getting off the bus,
in five minutes I'll be at your house.
c Where did you get this great/good-looking belt? –
I got it from my sister. She bought it in Munich.
d We had a flat tire. That's why we're just getting here
now. – No worries. You've still arrived early enough. We
haven't started yet.

**6   Translate into English.**
a Excuse me, how do I get to the train station, please? –
Go to the next intersection, turn right there and then
right again at the light.
b Bernd said we have to go around the playlot and then
along Schiller Street. – Yeah, but I think we went the
wrong way. We're on Goethe Street now.
c Can you scan with a cell phone, too? – Yes, nowadays
that's doable.
d Who accepted the package? – I don't know. The sig-
nature on the delivery slip is illegible.

**7   Translate into German.**
a Ich bin gleich fertig. Kannst du schon (mal) die
Fahrräder aus dem Keller holen? – Ja, aber mach schnell.

b Wo warst du denn? Du bist ja ganz rot im Gesicht! –
Ich komme vom Fußballspielen.
c Wie kommt man denn zur Bibliothek? – Gehen Sie
hier durch den Park und biegen Sie dann links ab.
Fahren Sie die Parkstraße entlang bis zur Ampel. Dort
biegen Sie rechts ab.
d Man kann eine Panne haben. Deshalb muss man
Werkzeug dabei haben.
e Warum brauchst du denn ein Wörterbuch? – Weil ich
diesen Text nicht verstehe.

**8   Translate into German.**
a Dieses Wasser kann man nicht trinken. Hast du das
Schild denn nicht gelesen? – Ach, es ist nicht trinkbar?
b Diese Pilze sehen sehr gut aus. Kann man sie essen? –
Nein, Vorsicht, die sind nicht essbar.
c Wie ist denn das Wetter bei euch in New York? Was
für Kleidung soll ich mitnehmen? – Es ist sonnig, aber
nimm einen Regenschirm mit. Vielleicht regnet es.

## Chapter 12

**5   Translate into English.**
a Are you all driving into the mountains again this year?
– No, we want to go to the coast, probably to the Baltic
Sea.
b The Müller family is moving. They bought a house in
the country. – Yes, they they'll also have more peace and
quiet than in the city.
c This year, Kurt doesn't just want to lie on the beach.
He'd like to do something completely different. – I can
understand that. We're taking a trip across the desert.
Why don't you all come along?

**6   Translate into English.**
a How long does a flight to Australia last? – Over 20
hours/more than 20 hours.
b Ms. Kleinfeld, from today on, please look after the
language classes again. – Oh, how happy that makes me!
c From 11 p.m. on, the busses don't run as often. –
I know. Maybe I can get a ride with Inge.

**7   Translate into German.**
a Am Wochenende könnten wir mal (wieder) an den
Strand (gehen / fahren). – Ach nein, ich langweile mich
am Strand. Warum fahren wir nicht in die Berge?
b Im Urlaub fahre ich an den Bodensee. Ich habe eine
schöne Pension mit Blick auf den See gefunden.
c Vermiete kleines Appartment in ruhiger Umgebung,
mit großer Terrasse und fantastischer Aussicht.

**8   Translate into German.**
a Wie war die Reise? – Gut, aber auch anstrengend. Der
Flug hat fünf Stunden gedauert und dann hatten wir
auch noch eine Stunde Verspätung.
b Ab dem ersten Januar halten die Busse 21 und 33
auch am Bahnhof. – Fahren sie auch am Mozartplatz
vorbei?

c Ich möchte bitte ein Einzelzimmer buchen. – Ja gern, für wann wäre das? – Für den dritten Mai. – Und für wie viele Nächte?

## Chapter 13

**4 Translate into English.**
a I don't know the word Bankleitzahl. Can you tell me what that means? – Sorry, I don't know either.
b Excuse me, do you know where the bus to Ismaning leaves from? – Yes, across from the train station.
c Do you know if we're supposed to do exercise 5, too? – Yeah, we should do that one, too.
d I forgot how to connect that. Can you help me? – I don't know if I can.

**5 Translate into English.**
a I lost my ID. – Then you have to have a new one issued.
b You need to have that suit cleaned. –Yes, that's true. Can you take it to the dry cleaners tomorrow?
c Let them give you a form in the registration office and fill it out. – What kind of form do I need?

**6 Translate into German.**
a Entschuldigung, kannst du mir sagen, wo die Aula 10 ist? – Ja, es ist die dritte Tür rechts.
b Ich weiß nicht mehr, ob wir morgen Unterricht haben. – Ja, bis eins.
c Entschuldigung, können Sie mir sagen, wie man zum Bahnhof kommt? – Tut mir leid, ich bin nicht von hier.
d Ich weiß nicht, ob ich ihnen meine E-Mail-Adresse geben soll. – Ich glaube, das ist kein Problem.

**7 Translate into German.**
a Morgen bringe ich das Auto in die Werkstatt. Ich muss das Öl wechseln lassen.
b Ich möchte diese Papiere übersetzen lassen. Kennst du jemanden? – Meine Schwester macht Übersetzungen.
c Wohin gehst du? – Zum Friseur. Ich will mir die Haare schneiden lassen.

## Chapter 14

**6 Translate into English.**
a When I was a child, my mother often read to me. Then, I did that with my children, too. – In our house, we sang a lot.
b We could go to the theater again, or would you rather see a movie? – I'd really like to go to the opera most of all. I've never been there.
c I liked the book. It's very funny. – Oh yeah? I didn't like it at all. I think the story is pretty unimaginative.

**7 Translate into English.**
a Tanja's been divorced twice, but in spite of that, she wants to marry again. – Have you already met her new boyfriend?
b Hm, the chocolate tastes good. May I have another little piece? – Of course. Here, take some!
c I think it's good when you can talk with your partner about everything. – Me too, but it's also important that you listen correctly.

**8 Translate into German.**
a Was ist passiert? – Ich habe mein Fahrrad repariert und habe mich dabei verletzt. – Sollen wir zum Arzt gehen?
b Als Kind wollte ich Musiker werden, aber dann bin ich Deutschlehrer geworden. – Konntest du nicht beides werden?
c Du solltest mit der U-Bahn fahren, heute ist viel Verkehr. – Du hast recht, aber ich würde lieber mit dem Auto fahren, das ist bequemer.

**9 Translate into German.**
a Ich muss sparen. Ich möchte mir ein Häuschen am Strand kaufen. – Wo willst du denn eins kaufen?
b Heute Abend ist ein Konzert im Konservatorium. Es ist kostenlos, um halb acht fängt es an. – Oh, da würde ich auch gerne hingehen. Sollen wir uns um sieben am Eingang treffen?
c Wie ist das Wetter jetzt an der Küste? – Es ist sehr windig und kalt, ein unangenehmes Wetter. – Na ja, es kann ja nicht immer nur sonnig sein.

## Lektion 8

### A

**1** **B** Text 4 **C** Text 2 **D** Text 1

**2** **b** Er kann dort mit den Kindern Fußball spielen. **c** Er muss in der Woche viel arbeiten. **d** Er kann da seine Freunde treffen.

**3** **b** …, weil er dort mit den Kindern Fußball spielen kann. **c** …, weil er in der Woche viel arbeiten muss. **d** …, weil er da seine Freunde treffen kann.

**4** **b** Trotzdem geht Familie Grimaldi an den Kirchweiler See. **c** Trotzdem sitzt Herr Windlich ungefähr drei Stunden im Garten. **d** Trotzdem geht Peter Lustig ins Schwimmbad.

**5** *Musterlösung*:
Am Freitagabend treffe ich mich am liebsten mit Freunden. Da gehen wir dann immer Fußball spielen. Am Samstag kann ich endlich mal lange schlafen und mal nichts tun. Sonntag mache ich gerne einen Ausflug oder ich treffe Freunde.

**6** **b** Ich fahre trotzdem in Urlaub. **c** Deine Tochter läuft trotzdem im T-Shirt herum. **d** Ich muss trotzdem gehen. **e** Ich gehe trotzdem mit dir ins Kino.

**7**

**b**

| Trotzdem | fahre | ich | in Urlaub. |
|---|---|---|---|
| Ich | fahre | trotzdem | in Urlaub. |

**c**

| Trotzdem | läuft | deine Tochter | im T-Shirt herum. |
|---|---|---|---|
| Deine Tochter | läuft | trotzdem | im T-Shirt herum. |

**8** **b** Trotzdem schaue ich mit meinen Freunden einen Videofilm an. **c** Trotzdem höre ich es mit dir an. **d** Trotzdem geht er nicht ins Bett. **e** Trotzdem isst er viel Süßes.

**9** *Musterlösung:*
Ich bin müde. Trotzdem gehe ich nicht ins Bett. Ich muss lernen. Trotzdem sehe ich lieber fern. Es regnet. Trotzdem gehe ich spazieren. Ich habe keine Lust. Trotzdem mache ich meine Hausaufgaben. Es kommt nichts Interessantes im Fernsehen. Trotzdem schalte ich den Fernseher nicht ab. Ich will nicht streiten. Trotzdem ärgere ich meinen Bruder.

### B

**10** **a** **2** Ich hätte lieber eine Katze. **3** Ich würde lieber ans Meer fahren.
   **b** **2** Ich hätte **3** Wir würden … fahren, wir würden … tanzen, wir würden … spazieren gehen

**11** **b** Ich würde lieber spazieren gehen. **c** Ich hätte gern mal ein bisschen Ruhe. **d** Ich wäre lieber gesund. **e** Ich würde lieber ans Meer fahren. **f** Ich wäre jetzt am liebsten in der Disco.

**12** **b** Ich würde lieber bei dir sein. **c** Er würde lieber mit Freunden ins Schwimmbad gehen. **d** Wir würden lieber auf dem Balkon sitzen. **e** Ich wäre lieber schon zu Hause. **f** Ich hätte lieber Urlaub.

**13** **b** Ich hätte auch gern frei. / Oh, da würde ich jetzt auch gern sitzen. **c** Oh, da wäre ich jetzt auch gern. / Oh, ich würde auch gern nach Brasilien fliegen. / Oh, da würde ich jetzt auch gern hinfliegen. **d** Oh, ich würde jetzt auch gern eine Wanderung machen. / Oh, ich würde heute auch gern wandern gehen.

**15** **b** achtzehn, Führerschein **c** Hamburg, Probleme **d** Verkäuferin, andere, Kindern

**17** Ich arbeite viel ➡ und komme immer sehr spät nach Hause. ➘ Am Wochenende ruhe ich mich aus. ➘ Bei schönem Wetter sitze ich im Garten ➡ und mache gar nichts. ➘ Und wenn am Abend ein guter Krimi im Fernsehen kommt, ➡ bin ich glücklich. ➘

### C

**19** **b** Du könntest ins Kino gehen. **c** Du könntest ihr Blumen schenken. **d** Du könntest am Samstag ins Stadion gehen. **e** Du könntest einen Ausflug machen.

**20** **a** 6 – 3 – 1 – 7 – 5 – 2 – 4   **b** 4 – 2 – 1 – 5 – 3 – 6

**21** **1** Lust – Idee – Wie wär's – Warum nicht – das geht bei mir – Also, dann
   **2** es tut mir sehr leid – Schade – trotzdem vielen Dank für die Einladung

**22** **b** Das ist ein guter Vorschlag. Da spielt Stuttgart gegen Hamburg. **c** Ich möchte lieber in die Disco gehen. **d** Ich komme leider nicht mit, ich war gestern schon auf dem Markt. **e** Warum nicht? Vielleicht können wir italienisch essen gehen.

**23** *Musterlösung:*
**a** Ich würde gern mit dir Tennis spielen. – Schade, das geht leider nicht. Ich bin krank. – Vielleicht können wir in zwei Wochen wieder zusammen spielen. **b** Wir könnten zusammen eine Wanderung machen. Hast du Lust? – Ja, gerne, wohin wollen wir denn gehen? **c** Ich würde gern mit dir schwimmen gehen. – Wie wäre es morgen Nachmittag? – Gut, wann genau sollen wir uns treffen? **d** Wir könnten am Donnerstagabend essen gehen. – Tut mir leid, da habe ich leider keine Zeit. – Na, dann vielleicht am Freitag? – Ja, das geht.

### D

**24**

| | gehen | bleiben | fahren | machen | besuchen | spielen | anschauen | schlafen |
|---|---|---|---|---|---|---|---|---|
| Tennis | | | | | | x | x | |
| Freunde | | x | | | x | | | |
| tanzen | x | | (x) | | | | | |
| einen Ausflug | | | | x | | | | |
| spazieren | x | | x | | | | | |
| bis elf Uhr | | x | | | | (x) | | x |
| ein Fußballspiel | | | | (x) | | x | x | |
| ins Schwimmbad | x | | x | | | | | |
| eine Radtour | | | | x | | | | |
| Skateboard | | | x | | | | | |
| zu Hause | | x | | | | x | x | x |

### E

**26** **a** Ausflug **b** Museum **c** Kino **d** Volkshochschule

**27** 1 b 2 a 3 c 4 a 5 b

## Lektion 9

### A

**1** **a** dick – dünn; groß – klein; hell – dunkel **b** lang – kurz; interessant – langweilig; neu – alt; schwer – leicht

**2** **b** klein **c** kurz **d** dick **e** groß **f** alt

**3** **a** die **b** der **c** das **d** die **e** die

**4**

| das Handy | Das ist … | ein | großes Handy. | -es |
|-----------|-----------|-----|---------------|-----|
| die Kette | | eine | lange Kette. | -e |
| die (viele) Bücher | Das sind … | - | interessante Bücher. | -e |
| | | keine | interessanten Bücher. | -en |

**5** **b** eine gute Lampe **c** ein billiges Buch **d** ein runder Tisch **e** bequeme Stühle

**6** **b** schönes **c** kleiner **d** alte **e** lange

**7** **b** Das sind keine großen Gläser, das sind kleine Gläser. **c** Das ist keine schwarze Jacke, das ist eine weiße Jacke. **d** Das ist kein altes Radio, das ist ein neues Radio. **e** Das ist keine billige Lampe, das ist eine teure Lampe. **f** Das sind keine neuen Löffel, das sind alte Löffel.

**8** **b** runden **c** gutes **d** alte **e** schöne

**9** **b** eine helle Lampe; helle Lampen **c** eine billige Kamera; billige Kameras **d** ein interessantes Buch; keine langweiligen Bücher; interessante Bücher

**10** **b** Haben Sie einen dicken Schal? – Nein, wir haben keine dicken Schals. / Nein, wir haben nur dünne Schals. **c** Haben Sie eine blaue Kanne? – Ja, selbstverständlich haben wir blaue Kannen. **d** Haben Sie ein braunes Regal? – Nein, wir haben keine braunen Regale. **e** Haben Sie eine gute Kaffeemaschine? – Ja, wir haben eine gute Kaffeemaschine. / gute Kaffeemaschinen. **f** Haben Sie eine schöne Zuckerdose? – Ja, wir haben eine schöne Zuckerdose. / schöne Zuckerdosen.

### B

**11** **b** in **c** mit **d** von **e** zu

**12** das Geschäft: in einem guten Geschäft; die Lampe: bei einer neuen Lampe; die Regale: zu meinen hellen Regalen

**13** **b** … mit großen Türen. **c** … mit einem flachen Bildschirm. **d** … mit kleinen und großen Löffeln? **e** … mit einer weichen Sohle.

**14**

| | Stoff | Holz | Glas | Metall | Papier | Plastik |
|---------|-------|------|------|--------|--------|---------|
| Spielzeug | x | x | | x | | x |
| Flaschen | | | x | | | x |
| Kleider | x | | | | | |
| Möbel | x | x | x | x | | x |
| Fenster | | x | x | x | | x |
| Autos | x | | | x | | x |
| Bücher | | | | | x | |

**15** **b** einen neuen Wecker **c** große Wecker **d** einen kleinen Wecker **e** kleine Wecker **f** einen großen Wecker **g** schöne Wecker **h** einen lauten Wecker **i** alte Wecker **j** einen neuen Wecker **k** einen nicht zu großen **l** nicht zu kleinen **m** nicht zu leisen **n** nicht zu alten Wecker **o** einem hellen Licht **p** ein neues Handy

**20** Wir kaufen

den Schrank.
einen großen Schrank.
die großen Schränke.
große Schränke.
keine großen Schränke.

Der Tisch steht neben

dem Schrank.
einem großen Schrank.
den großen Schränken.
großen Schränken.

…

### C

**21** **b** jung – jünger – am jüngsten **c** schön – schöner – am schönsten **d** gesund – gesünder – am gesündesten **e** leicht – leichter – am leichtesten **f** hoch – höher – am höchsten **g** gut – besser – am besten **h** dunkel – dunkler – am dunkelsten **i** lang – länger – am längsten **j** lieb – lieber – am liebsten **k** groß – größer – am größten **l** teuer – teurer – am teuersten **m** interessant – interessanter – am interessantesten **n** viel – mehr – am meisten

**22** **b** leichter … am leichtesten **c** besser … am besten **d** länger als ein Bus … am längsten **e** höher … am höchsten **f** gesünder … am gesündesten **g** jünger … am jüngsten **h** billiger … am billigsten **i** größer … am größten ist unser Pferd.

**23** *Musterlösung:*
**a** Der Philips ist größer als der Sharp, aber der Thomson ist am größten. Der Philips ist kleiner als der Thomson, aber der Sharp ist am kleinsten. **b** Der Philips ist schwerer als der Sharp, aber der Thomson ist am schwersten. Der Philips ist leichter als der Thomson, aber der Sharp ist am leichtesten. **c** Der Sharp ist teurer als der Philips, aber der Thomson ist am teuersten. Der Sharp ist billiger als der Thomson, aber der Philips ist am billigsten. **d** Der Thomson gefällt mir besser als der Sharp, aber der Philips gefällt mir am besten. Der Thomson gefällt mir weniger als der Philips, aber der Sharp gefällt mir am wenigsten.

**24** **b** älter **c** besser **d** billiger **e** schneller

**25** **b** Die Zugspitze ist ein hoher Berg, der Großglockner ist höher, aber am höchsten ist das Matterhorn. **c** Die Elbe ist ein langer Fluss, der Rhein ist länger, aber am längsten ist die Donau. **d** Genf ist eine große Stadt, Wien ist größer, aber am größten ist Berlin. / Genf hat viele Einwohner, Wien hat mehr Einwohner (als Genf), aber Berlin hat am/die meisten Einwohner. **e** Preis: Das Auto ist billiger als das Flugzeug, aber am billigsten ist der Zug. Dauer: Eine Fahrt mit dem Zug dauert länger als mit dem Auto, aber am schnellsten ist/geht es mit dem Flugzeug.

**26** **b** feiner **c** elegant **d** günstig **e** leichter **f** schöner **g** flachen; tiefe **h** hoch

**27** **b** als **c** als **d** wie **e** als

### D

**27** **b** Kredit **c** Miete **d** Qualität **e** Auto **f** Musikanlage **g** Urlaub **h** Bildschirm **i** Form **j** Fernsehgerät **k** Nahrungsmittel **l** Handy **m** Versicherung

**28** **b** so viel Geld **c** so gern wie **d** so gut wie

**29** **b** wie **c** wie **d** als **e** wie

# Answers to the Workbook Exercises

## E

**30**

**a**

| Bild | 1 | 2 | 3 |
|---|---|---|---|
| Text | C | A | B |

**b**

| Name | Gegen-stand | Aussehen | Von wem bekommen? | Wann bekommen? | Warum ist das der Lieb-lingsgegen-stand? |
|---|---|---|---|---|---|
| Sascha | *Kinder-schuh* | *klein, blau* | *von seiner Freundin* | *letztes Jahr* | *Den anderen Schuh hat seine Freun-din, beide Schuhe ge-hören zusam-men so wie seine Freundin und er.* |
| Conny | *Uhr* | *alt, sehr schön* | *von ihrem Opa* | *vor zwei Jahren* | *Erinnert sie an ihre Oma.* |
| Pauline | *Gitarre* | *—-* | *selbst gekauft* | *mit 14 Jahren* | *Es geht ihr gut, wenn sie Gitarre spielt.* |

## Lektion 10

### A

**1** **b** Die Fenster werden geputzt. **c** Der Briefträger sortiert die Briefe. **d** Die Briefe werden sortiert. **e** Herr Maier repariert sein Auto. **f** Das Auto wird in der Werkstatt repariert.

**2** **a** 1 sortiert 2 gewogen 3 verpackt 4 transportiert
**b**

| | | | | |
|---|---|---|---|---|
| 1 | die Äpfel | werden | Zuerst | sortiert. |
| 2 | Dann | werden | sie | gewogen. |
| 3 | Hier | werden | sie | verpackt. |
| 4 | Schließlich | werden | sie in den Supermarkt | transportiert. |

**3** **a** wird **b** wird **c** werden **d** wird **e** werden

**4** **b** Auf der Post wird das Päckchen gewogen. **c** Der Päck-chenschein wird ausgefüllt. **d** Das Päckchen wird verschickt. **e** Das Päckchen wird mit dem Flugzeug transportiert. **f** Es wird zu Marias Schwester gebracht.

**6** **b – p** Bleib: p; Schreibst: p; schreibe: b; bald: b
**d – t** sind: t; freundlich: t; leid: t; Leider: d; bald: t
**g – k** regnet: g; Sag: k; sage: g; Zeigen: g

### B

**10** **b** der runde Tisch **c** die neue Kamera **d** das teure Handy **e** der langweilige Film **f** die faule Angestellte **g** die kurze Hose

**11** **b** ▲ Schau mal, wie gefällt dir denn die weiße Uhr?
● Nicht so gut, die gelbe gefällt mir besser.
**c** ▲ Schau mal, wie gefällt dir denn das blaue Handy?
● Nicht so gut, das schwarze gefällt mir besser.
**d** ▲ Schau mal, wie gefällt dir denn der schwarze Computer?
● Nicht so gut, der graue gefällt mir besser.

**e** ▲ Schau mal, wie gefallen dir denn die roten Handy-taschen?
● Nicht so gut, die schwarzen gefallen mir besser.

**12** **b** den kleinen schwarzen Fernseher **c** die neuen Kameras; die schwarze **d** die verrückten Handytaschen

**13** **a** mit dem neuen Gürtel **b** mit den weißen Blumen **c** die blaue Jeans mit dem weißen T-Shirt **d** die weiße Jacke **e** den schwarzen Rock mit der roten Bluse **f** die neue Handtasche

**14** *Musterlösung:*

| | maskulin der | neutral das | feminin die | Plural die |
|---|---|---|---|---|
| Mir gefällt / gefallen … | der graue Computer | das schwarze Handy | die gelbe Uhr | die schwarzen Handytaschen |
| Ich will … | den schwarzen Fernseher | das gelbe Radio | die schwarze Kamera | die verrückten Handytaschen |
| mit … | dem neuen Gürtel | dem weißen T-Shirt | der roten Bluse | den weißen Blumen |

**15** **a** alten **b** teuren; guten; neuen **c** anderen; weiße; hellen; dünnen **d** kleinen; gute; aktuelle

**16** **b** der gelben Jacke. **c** den weißen Streifen! **d** den roten Punkten? **e** der blaue Anzug?

**17** *Musterlösung:*
**b** Ich möchte für meine 30-jährige Freundin ein Brettspiel.
**c** Ich möchte ein neues Kleid für ein Hochzeitsfest.
**d** Ich möchte ein Stofftier als Geburtstagsgeschenk für ein 6-jähriges Mädchen.

### C

**18** **b** eine **c** – **d** ein **e** einen

**19** **b** Was für ein T-Shirt? **c** Was für Schuhe … **d** Was für einen … **e** Was für eine …

**20** **b** auf einen Anrufbeantworter sprechen **c** ein Visum beantragen **d** einen Termin verschieben **e** den Ausweis beantragen **f** eine SMS schicken

**21** **a** Aber ich musste bei der Reinigung etwas abholen. **b** … ich zu einer Untersuchung gehen musste. **c** … ich hatte ein Treffen mit meinen Kollegen. **d** … ich musste im Konsulat meinen Ausweis verlängern.

**23** **a** Liebe Claudia,
gerade habe ich einen Anruf von meinem Vater bekommen. Meine Mutter liegt im Krankenhaus. Es tut mir sehr leid, dass ich nicht kommen kann. Natürlich will ich heute Abend meine Mutter besuchen. Vielleicht könnten wir unser Treffen verschieben?
Viele Grüße
…

**b** *Musterlösung:*
Liebe Andrea,
vor ein paar Stunden habe ich überraschend Besuch von meinen Eltern bekommen. Sie wollen bis übermorgen bleiben. Deshalb kann ich leider nicht zu unserer Verabredung kommen. Können wir unser Treffen vielleicht verschieben? Wann hast du wieder Zeit? Schreib mir doch einfach!
Viele Grüße
…

**D**

**24** **a** Person 1: negativ; **Person 2:** positiv; **Person 3:** positiv;
**Person 4:** negativ
**b** 1 falsch 2 richtig 3 richtig 4 richtig

**25**

| problemlos ohne *Problem* | fehlerlos ohne *Fehler* | phantasielos ohne *Phantasie* |
|---|---|---|
| ruhelos ohne *Ruhe* | arbeitslos ohne *Arbeit* | fleischlos ohne *Fleisch* |
| planlos ohne *Plan* | kinderlos ohne *Kinder* | pausenlos ohne *Pause* |

**26** **b** arbeitslos **c** unmöglich **d** unfreundlich **e** unwichtig
**f** unmodern **g** problemlos

**E**

**28** **b** auffordern **c** erwarten **d** die Übung **e** entscheiden **f** die
Reinigung **g** (sich) entschuldigen **h** besorgen **i** die Meinung
**j** wohnen **k** die Untersuchung **l** (sich) unterhalten **m** beraten
**n** die Empfehlung

**29** **b** Wohnung **c** meinst **d** untersucht **e** entschuldigen
**f** Reinigung **g** entscheiden; empfehlen

**30** **a** Kommunikation **b** Missverständnis **c** Kontinente
**d** Konferenz **e** Beziehung **f** Notiz **g** Sekunden

# Lektion 11

**A**

**1** **a** 2 beim Metzger, in der Metzgerei 3 bei meiner Oma, in
der Parkstraße 18 4 bei Freunden, im Hainweg 2
**b** 2 zum Metzger, in die Metzgerei 3 zu meiner Oma, in
die Parkstraße 18 4 zu Freunden, in den Hainweg 2

**2** **b** vom Metzger, aus/von der Metzgerei **c** von meiner Oma,
aus der Parkstraße 18 **d** von Freunden, aus dem Hainweg 2

**3** **a** auf dem, vom **b** zum, beim, vom **c** ins, im, aus dem
**d** auf den, auf dem, vom **e** in den, im, aus dem

**4** **b** vom Reisebüro **c** ins Reisebüro **d** aus dem Reisebüro **e** auf
den Fußballplatz **f** vom Fußballplatz **g** in die Post **h** aus der
Post **j** von der Post

**5** **b** … vom Bäcker. **c** … komme gerade von der Tankstelle.
**d** Ja, ich komme gerade vom Supermarkt. **e** Ja, ich komme
gerade vom Frisör.

**6** *Musterlösung:*
Um 13 Uhr muss er Jana von der Schule abholen. Um 14
Uhr muss er Pauli vom Kindergarten abholen. Um 15 Uhr
muss er Jana zur Geburtstagsfeier von Claudia bringen. Um
16 Uhr muss er Pauli zu Daniel bringen. Um ca. 18 Uhr
muss er Jana von der Geburtstagsfeier abholen, vorher muss
er noch Pauli von Daniel abholen.

**B**

**8** 6 – 3 – 8 – 1 – 4 – 5 – 2 – 7

**9** **b** gegenüber vom **c** die Poststraße entlang **d** durch die, bis
zur, rechts **e** am, um das

**10** *Musterlösung:*
**b** Dann ist er an der Ampel links gegangen und an
der nächsten Ecke gleich wieder rechts abgebogen.
Danach ist er die Auenstraße entlang gelaufen bis zur
Friedrichstraße. Dort ist er nach links gegangen. An der
nächsten Ampel ist er wieder nach rechts gegangen.

**c** Dann muss er nach rechts gehen und die Friedrichstraße entlang gehen bis zur Paulstraße. Dort muss er
links in die Paulstraße abbiegen und bis zur zweiten
Straße auf der rechten Seite gehen. Das ist der
Kirchweg. Dort wohnt sein Freund im zweiten Haus auf
der linken Seite.

**11** **b** über den Marktplatz / durch diese Straße fahren **c** in die
Straße hineinfahren / links abbiegen **d** weiterfahren
**e** auf der rechten Straßenseite parken

**C**

**13** **b** Ich bringe es in die Werkstatt. **c** Ich gehe zur Bank.
**d** Ich mache eine Pause. **e** Ich lege mich ins Bett.

**14** **b** Deshalb bringe ich es in die Werkstatt. **c** Deshalb gehe ich
zur Bank. **d** Deshalb mache ich eine Pause. **e** Deshalb lege
ich mich ins Bett.

**15** **a** Vorderlicht **b** Bremse **c** Reifen **d** Klingel
**e** Rücklicht **f** Werkzeug

**16** **a** 2 … weil man bei Nacht gut sehen muss. 3 … weil man
manchmal eine Panne hat. 4 … weil man manchmal
andere Radfahrer überholen möchte.

**b**

| **2** *Man muss bei Nacht gut sehen.* | *Deshalb* | *braucht* | *man* | *ein helles Vorderlicht.* |
|---|---|---|---|---|
| | *Man* | *braucht* | *deshalb* | *ein helles Vorderlicht.* |
| **3** Man hat manchmal eine Panne. | *Deshalb* | *braucht* | *man* | *Werkzeug.* |
| | *Man* | *braucht* | *deshalb* | *Werkzeug.* |
| **4** Man möchte manchmal andere Rad-fahrer über-holen. | *Deshalb* | *braucht* | *man* | *eine gute Klingel.* |
| | *Man* | *braucht* | *deshalb* | *eine gute Klingel.* |

**17** **b** deshalb **c** deshalb **d** weil **e** deshalb **f** denn

**18** **b** hörbar **c** erkennbar **d** bezahlbar **e** abschließbar

**19** Motor: A; Bremse: A, F; Benzin: A; Rücklicht: A, F; Garage:
A, F; Tankstelle: A; Werkstatt: A, F; Klingel: F; Panne: A, F;
Vorderlicht: A, F; Werkzeug: A, F

**22** *z* oder *tz*

**23** 2, 4, 5, 7, 9

**D**

**24** **b** der Regen **c** das Eis **d** das Gewitter **f** der Nebel **g** die
Sonne **h** der Wind

**25** **a** gewittrige, Sonne und Wolken, 17 Grad im Norden,
29 Grad im Süden, starker Westwind

**b**

| Wie wird das Wetter? | im Norden | in der Mitte | im Süden |
|---|---|---|---|
| heute Nacht | weniger Regen 10–15 Grad | 10–15 Grad | 10–15 Grad |
| am Dienstag | Wolken, einzelne Schauer oder Gewitter 17 Grad | zunächst viel Sonnen-schein | einige dickere Wolken meist freundlich bis 29 Grad |

**26** **b** 3

**c**

| Mail 2 | Das Wetter ist schön. | Er kann Regenschirm und warme Kleidung zu Hause lassen. |
|---|---|---|
| Mail 3 | Alles ist möglich: Sonne, Regen, Schnee. | Er soll Sachen für gutes und schlechtes Wetter mitnehmen. |

**d** Lieber Herr Tsara,
im Moment ist bei uns leider schlechtes Wetter. Es schneit und die Temperaturen liegen bei minus 5 Grad. Es ist also ganz schön kalt. Nehmen Sie deshalb am besten warme Kleidung und einen dicken Wintermantel mit.
Beste Grüße
...

**27** Senkrecht:
1 Bushaltestelle 2 Fahrer 3 Boot 4 PKW 6 Führerschein 7 Bahnhof 8 Ampel 9 Stau 10 landen 11 Parkplatz 12 spazieren 13 transportieren 14 Verspätung
Waagerecht:
1 Auto 2 starten 4 Fahrkarte 5 verkehr 6 Motor 7 Fahrrad 8 Polizei 9 Reparatur 10 unterwegs

**28**

| | nehmen | umsteigen | fahren | einsteigen | gehen | aussteigen |
|---|---|---|---|---|---|---|
| **b** in den Zug | | x | | x | | |
| **c** am Goetheplatz | | x | | x | | x |
| **d** aus dem Bus | | | | | | x |
| **e** das Fahrrad | x | | | | | |
| **f** zu Fuß | | | | | x | |
| **g** mit dem Schiff | | | x | | | |
| **h** spazieren | | | | | x | |
| **i** über die Brücke | | | x | | x | |
| **j** über Traunstadt | | | x | | | |

**29** 1 Michaelikirche c; 2 Rathaus e; 3 Stadtmuseum h; 4 Stadtpark i; 5 Stadtcafé j

## Lektion 12

### A

**1**

| | Wo? Sie ist ... | Wohin? Sie fährt ... | Woher? Sie kommt ... |
|---|---|---|---|
| **a** | in Italien. | nach Italien. | aus Italien. |
| **b** | in der Schweiz. | in die Schweiz. | aus der Schweiz. |
| **c** | im Kino. | ins Kino. | aus dem Kino. |
| **d** | bei Claudia. | zu Claudia. | von Claudia. |
| **e** | beim Arzt. | zum Arzt. | vom Arzt. |

**2** **a** zu, in der **b** nach, in, in die **c** zum, beim **d** ins, zu

**3** 1 der Berg 2 das Gebirge 3 die Insel 4 die Küste 5 der Norden 6 der Osten 7 der Wald 8 der See 9 das Meer 10 der Strand

**4** **a** 1 *an*: der Rhein, der Titisee, der Strand, das Meer
2 *auf*: die Insel, das Land 3 *in*: das Gebirge, die Berge, die Wüste, der Schwarzwald, der Süden
**b** 1 an den Titisee. 2 im Gebirge. 3 in der Wüste. 4 in den Süden. 5 an den Strand? 6 an der Atlantikküste.

**5** **b** Bild 4 **c** Bild 5 **d** Bild 1 **e** Bild 3 **f** Bild 6

**6**

| | Wo? | Wohin? | Woher? |
|---|---|---|---|
| **b** | in der Wüste | in die Wüste | aus der Wüste |
| **c** | an der Küste | an die Küste | von der Küste |
| **d** | auf der Insel | auf die Insel | von der Insel |
| **e** | in Berlin | nach Berlin | aus Berlin |
| **f** | in der Türkei | in die Türkei | aus der Türkei |
| **g** | am Chiemsee | an den Chiemsee | vom Chiemsee |
| **h** | am Strand | an den Strand | vom Strand |
| **i** | im Gebirge | ins Gebirge | aus dem Gebirge |
| **j** | im Wald | in den Wald | aus dem Wald |

**7** nach, ans, im, am, zum, vom, im, aus, nach

**8** bei, am, im, auf, von, zu, ins, ins

**10** **a** windig **b** gefährlich **c** anstrengend **d** trocken

### B

**11** **A** kinderliebe, vielen, wuderbarer, eigenem, eigener **B** Schöne, moderne, ruhiger **C** Großes **D** lauten, Schöne, große, schönem, Gutes, guter

**12**

| (der) | (das) | (die) | (die) |
|---|---|---|---|
| schöner Spielplatz | ruhiges Haus | ruhige Lage | kinderliebe Tiere |
| ohne lauten Verkehr | großes Zelt | schöne Landschaft | moderne Wohnungen |
| mit schönem Blick | mit eigenem Bad | mit eigener Küche | mit vielen Frei-zeitmöglich-keiten |

**13** **a** kleines **b** Günstige, großem, großer, tierliebe **c** ruhige, günstiger, netter **d** Kleines, ruhigen, historischem

**14** *Musterlösung:*
**a** Urlaub auf dem Bauernhof: Schöne, günstige Ferien-wohnungen in ruhiger Lage an tierliebe Gäste zu vermieten! Die Zimmer haben Balkon mit Blick aufs Gebirge und den Fluss.
**b** Ruhiger und sauberer Campingplatz direkt am See! Schiffe mieten möglich. Spielplatz für die Kinder vorhanden.
**c** Modernes, kinderfreundliches Hotel in bester Lage: Von den Balkons aus können Sie den Strand sehen, außerdem ist ein großes Schwimmbad vorhanden. Dies alles bieten wir zum günstigen Preis.

### C

**15** **a** Montag bis Freitag von 10 Uhr bis 18.30 Uhr ... am Samstag ... um 14 Uhr **b** Am Freitag. ... Bis Montag früh ... für drei Nächte. **c** ... im Herbst ... im Oktober **d** Am 13. Februar.

**16** **a** Seit **b** Vor **c** Nach **d** vor **e** Seit

**17** **a** ab, ohne **b** über, von ... an, Über

**18** Was kostet das? – Wie lange dauert denn die Busfahrt? – Fahren die Busse täglich? – Gibt es denn noch freie Plätze? – Für wie viele Personen möchten Sie buchen?

### D

**19** jemand einladen: Bitte komm mich doch besuchen! Ich würde mich sehr freuen! Ich möchte dich gern nach ... einladen.

<u>Vorschläge machen:</u> Wir könnten … fahren. Ich könnte dir … zeigen. Hier kannst du auch … besichtigen.
<u>nach Wünschen fragen:</u> Wofür interessierst du dich? Möchtest du gern …? Hast du Lust auf einen Besuch in …? Was möchtest du gern machen?

**20** ins Kino gehen, mit dem Schiff fahren, ins Museum gehen, in eine Kneipe gehen, einen Ausflug machen, ins Fußballstadion gehen

**21** wie, würde, nach, an den, außerhalb, gibt es, anschauen/besichtigen, auf, dir, Grüße

**22** *Musterlösung:*
Liebe Angela,
vielen Dank für deine Einladung. Ich habe mich sehr darüber gefreut. Natürlich komme ich dich gerne besuchen, ich war nämlich noch nie in Wien. Ich möchte gerne das Schloss besichtigen und Schiff fahren, die Idee finde ich echt super! Auch die Kaffeehäuser möchte ich mir gerne ansehen.
Ach ja, noch eine Frage: Darf meine Schwester auch mitkommen? Also, dann bis bald in Wien.
Herzliche Grüße
Maria

**23** *Musterlösung:*
Liebe Angela,
danke für deine Karte und die Einladung nach Wien. Ich würde dich sehr gern besuchen, aber leider passt es im Moment nicht so gut. Ich habe nämlich gerade eine neue Stelle gefunden und bekomme noch keinen Urlaub. Aber vielleicht kannst du ja zu mir nach Hamburg kommen? Ich könnte dir die Stadt und den Hafen zeigen. Hast du Lust? Schreib mir bitte.
Viele Grüße
…

**25** Boot, von See zu See, seltene Vögel, Natur und Ruhe, ohne Lärm, Ferienwohnungen, modern und gemütlich, Zwei- und Drei-Zimmer-Apartments, Preis, ab 15 Euro

**26** <u>a</u>  Ich sage vier: → I In Köln ein Bier. ↘ II Ich sage überhaupt nichts mehr. ↘ II Ich staune nur: → I Da ist das Meer. ↘ II

    <u>b</u>  In Hamburg leben zwei Ameisen, → I  Die wollen nach Australien reisen. ↘ II Bei Altona auf der Chaussee, → I Da tun ihnen schon die Beine weh. ↘ II  Und da verzichten sie weise → I  Dann auf den letzten Teil der Reise. ↘ II

**E**

**27** <u>a</u>  Abenteuerurlaub: wilde Natur, durch die Wüste fahren, Dschungel, verrückte Leute, Risiko
    <u>b</u>  Kultururlaub: Museen besichtigen, ein Schloss besichtigen
    <u>c</u>  Erholungsurlaub: faul sein, am Strand liegen, kein Stress
    <u>d</u>  Sporturlaub: fit sein, Fußball spielen, täglich joggen, im Gebirge wandern, einen Tenniskurs machen, Radtour im Gebirge

**28** <u>a</u> richtig <u>b</u> falsch <u>c</u> falsch

**30** <u>a</u> Es regnet. <u>b</u> Seine Mutter anrufen. <u>c</u> Es gibt ein Tier auf der Autobahn.

## Lektion 13

**A**

**1** <u>a</u> Bank <u>b</u> Geld abheben <u>c</u> Kreditkarte; Telefonkarte <u>d</u> Service-Nummer

**2** <u>b</u> Wie alt bist du denn? <u>c</u> Wann kommst du nach Hause? <u>d</u> Wie viel Geld haben wir noch? <u>e</u> Wie lange dauert der Film? <u>f</u> Was bedeutet dieses Wort? <u>g</u> Wo hast du das gefunden?

**3** Kannst du mir sagen, / Können Sie mir sagen …

| | | | | |
|---|---|---|---|---|
| <u>b</u> 1 | Wie alt | bist | du? | |
| 2 | … wie alt | du | bist? | |
| <u>c</u> 1 | Wann | kommst | du nach Hause? | |
| 2 | … wann | | du nach Hause | kommst? |
| <u>d</u> 1 | Wie viel Geld | haben | wir noch? | |
| 2 | … wie viel  Geld | | wir noch | haben? |
| <u>e</u> 1 | Wie lange | dauert | der Film? | |
| 2 | … wie lange | | der Film | dauert? |
| f 1 | | Was | bedeutet | dieses Wort? |
| 2 | … was | | dieses Wort | bedeutet? |
| g 1 | Wo | hast | du das | gefunden? |
| 2 | … wo | | du das | gefunden hast? |

**4** <u>b</u> …, was du gerade machst. <u>c</u> …, wann du den gekauft hast. <u>d</u> …, wo du ihn gekauft hast. <u>e</u> …, wie man so ein Ding bloß anschließt.

**5** <u>b</u> Weißt du, wie spät es ist? <u>c</u> Woher kommst du ? <u>d</u> Ich frage mich, wie lange diese Übung noch dauert. <u>e</u> Wie geht es Ihnen?

**6** <u>b</u> wo Sie wohnen. <u>c</u> wann Sie geboren sind. <u>d</u> wo Sie geboren sind. <u>e</u> welche Staatsangehörigkeit Sie haben. <u>f</u> wie Ihre Telefonnummer ist.

**7** Weißt du schon, → wann du kommst? ↘ • Kommst du heute ↗ oder erst morgen? ↘ Sag mir bitte, → wo wir uns treffen. ↘ • Treffen wir uns um sechs ↗ oder lieber erst später? ↘ Kannst du mir sagen, → wie man das schreibt? ↘ • Schreibt man das mit „h" ↗ oder ohne „h"? ↘ Ich frage mich, → warum du so schlecht gelaunt bist. ↘ • Hast du ein Problem ↗ oder bist du nur müde? ↘

**8** …, welches Formular ich ausfüllen muss? …, wie spät es ist? … wo du das gesehen hast? …, wie ich die Übung machen soll? …, wann Herr Müller da ist? …, wo es einen Geldautomaten gibt? …, was der Brief kostet? …, wann die Bank geöffnet hat? …, warum du nie Zeit für mich hast? …, was dieses Wort bedeutet? …, wo ich unterschreiben muss?

**B**

**9** <u>b</u> Nein, wir nehmen nur Bargeld. <u>c</u> Nein! Erst, wenn du in der Schule besser wirst. <u>d</u> Nein, es sind noch 5 Euro übrig.

**10** <u>b</u> …, ob ich das Eis mit EC-Karte bezahlen kann? <u>c</u> …, ob ich diesen Monat mehr Geld bekomme. <u>d</u> …, ob du das ganze Geld ausgegeben hast.

**11**

| Ich wollte fragen, | ob | ich das Eis mit EC-Karte | bezahlen kann? |
|---|---|---|---|
| Papa, ich möchte dich fragen, | ob | ich diesen Monat, mehr Geld | bekomme. |
| Ich möchte wissen, | ob | du das ganze Geld | ausgegeben hast. |

**12** **b** ob man Schüler/in oder Student/in oder Auszubildende/r ist. **c** ob man Hausfrau oder Hausmann ist. **d** ob man arbeitslos ist. **e** ob man verheiratet oder geschieden ist.

**13** **b** wann **c** ob **d** wie lange **e** ob **f** wo **g** wie

**14** **b** ob die EC-Karte etwas kostet. **c** ob alle EC-Karten eine Geheimnummer haben. **d** ob die Bank viele Geldautomaten hat. **e** man mit der EC-Karte überall Geld bekommt.

**15** *Musterlösung:*
- ● Entschuldigen Sie, darf ich Sie etwas fragen?
- ■ Ja, natürlich. Womit kann ich Ihnen helfen?
- ● Ich möchte wissen, ob ich einen Fernseher kaufen kann, wenn ich nicht genug Geld habe.
- ■ Das macht nichts. Wir akzeptieren auch Kreditkarten.

- ■ Entschuldigen Sie, ich habe eine Frage.
- ● Ja, was kann ich für Sie tun?
- ■ Ich habe nur meine Kreditkarte dabei und möchte wissen, ob ich damit hier bezahlen kann.
- ● Ja, selbstverständlich.

- ● Entschuldigung, können Sie mir helfen?
- ■ Ja, natürlich. Was kann ich für Sie tun?
- ● Ich habe meine Geheimnummer vergessen und möchte wissen, ob ich auch ohne sie Geld abheben kann.
- ■ Ja, das ist möglich. Sagen Sie mir bitte Ihre Kontonummer.

- ■ Entschuldigen Sie, darf ich Sie etwas fragen?
- ● Ja, gerne.
- ■ Ich habe ein Eis gekauft und möchte wissen, ob ich auch mit EC-Karte bezahlen kann.
- ● Ein Eis mit EC-Karte? Also nein, das geht wirklich nicht.

**16** **a** Münzen **b** Bank, Zinsen **c** überweise **d** leihen **e** Zoll **f** bar **g** ausgeben **h** Kontonummer, Bankleitzahl

**C**

**18** die Wohnung putzen; das Fahrrad reparieren; ein Formular unterschreiben; (einen Text lesen); das Kleid reinigen

**19** **b** ..., er lässt sie putzen. **c** ..., ich lasse es ihn unterschreiben. **d** ..., ich lasse es immer reparieren. **e** Ich lasse es reinigen.

**20** **b** ..., dann musst du dir eine neue ausstellen lassen. – Gut, ich lasse mir eine neue ausstellen. **c** ... sie schneiden lassen. – Gut, ich lasse sie schneiden. **d** ... es reparieren lassen. – Gut, ich lasse es reparieren.

**21** **b** uns **c** mir **d** euch **e** sich **f** sich

**22** **b** lasse **c** lassen **d** lassen **e** Lasst **f** lässt

**23** *Musterlösung:*
... öffnen lassen. Am Mittwoch habe ich mir Rotwein über meine Jacke geschüttet und musste sie reinigen lassen. Am Donnerstag habe ich mir meine Hose zerrissen und musste sie nähen lassen. Am Freitag habe ich mich am Arm verletzt und musste mich beim Arzt untersuchen lassen. Am Samstag konnte ich mich deshalb nicht duschen und musste mir die Haare (von meiner Frau) waschen lassen.

**24** *Musterlösung:*
... und zu einem Seminar in Leipzig fahren. Außerdem muss ich mich an der VHS für den nächsten Deutschkurs anmelden. Jeden Monat am 30. muss ich die Miete überweisen. Nächsten Monat muss ich die Wohnung renovieren lassen und zum Sportfest von meinen Kindern gehen. Ich muss auch meine Zähne untersuchen lassen und habe deshalb einen Termin beim Zahnarzt. Und meine Haare muss ich auch schneiden lassen! Im August habe ich Urlaub. Da muss ich gar nichts machen.

**25** **b** falsch sind: *schüner* und *dümer*, richtig sind: *schöner* und *dümmer*

**D**

**26** **a** irgendwelche **b** irgendwo **c** irgendwas **d** irgendwelche **e** irgendwann **f** irgendwer

**27** **a** A – 2, B – 1, C – 3
**b** Text B

**E**

**28**

# Answers to the Workbook Exercises

## Lektion 14

### A

**1** **a** sollte, wollte **b** Durftet, mussten **c** Musstest, durften **d** Hattest, war, wollte, war

**2** **b** bin … gefallen; habe … verletzt; … liegen musste **c** bin … aufgewachsen **d** haben … mitgearbeitet **e** … eingekauft haben; haben … bekommen **f** hat … erzählt **g** bin … gefahren; hat … gefallen

**3** *Musterlösung:*
**b** Katrin hat oft mit ihren Eltern im Garten gearbeitet. **c** Nachmittags hat sie oft mit den Jungs aus dem Dorf Fußball gespielt. **d** Sie durfte im Sommer Würstchen über dem Lagerfeuer braten. **e** Sie ist gern zusammen mit ihrer Freundin auf Bäume geklettert.

### B

**4** **a** Ich würde jetzt gern in Ruhe Zeitung lesen. **b** Ich möchte jetzt gern allein sein. / Ich wäre jetzt gern allein. **c** Ich hätte gern ein neues Fahrrad. / Ich möchte gern ein neues Fahrrad. **d** Ich würde jetzt gern in Urlaub fahren. **e** Ich würde gern weniger arbeiten. **f** Ich möchte bei meinem Freund wohnen. / Ich würde gern bei meinem Freund wohnen.

**5** **a**

|   |         | schlechte Noten | Urlaub mit Eltern | Aussehen | der Freund |
|---|---------|-----------------|-------------------|----------|------------|
| 1 | Michael | x               |                   |          |            |
| 2 | Sonja   |                 |                   |          | x          |
| 3 | Arnold  |                 | x                 |          |            |
| 4 | Elisa   |                 |                   | x        |            |

**b** *Musterlösung:*
Du solltest offen mit deinen Eltern reden. Vielleicht solltest du sie zum Essen einladen und dann alles mit ihnen besprechen. Du könntest auch erst einmal ein wenig abwarten. Vielleicht kann dir auch sonst jemand aus der Familie helfen. In jedem Fall solltest du mehr lernen und im neuen Schuljahr Nachhilfe nehmen.

### C

**6** **a** richtig **b** falsch **c** falsch **d** richtig

**7** **a** ruhig, unruhig, ruhelos **b** arbeitslos, Arbeiter, Arbeiterin **c** Erziehung, erziehbar, Erzieher, Erzieherin **d** Kündigung, kündbar, unkündbar

**8** **a** lösbar **b** pausenlos **c** sonnig **d** Stückchen **e** Entscheidung **f** kündbar **g** unmöglich **h** kostenlos **i** Kätzchen **j** unhöflich

**9** **b** die Kleider, der Schrank, der Kleiderschrank **c** das Geschenk, das Papier, das Geschenkpapier **d** das Auto, der Schlüssel, der Autoschlüssel **f** das Telefon, das Buch, das Telefonbuch **e** der Garten, der Stuhl, der Gartenstuhl

### D

**10** **a** … gut versteht. **b** …, wenn man sich nach einem Streit immer wieder verzeiht. **c** Liebe ist, wenn man den anderen mit Geschenken überrascht. **d** Liebe ist, wenn man im Alltag noch gemeinsam Spaß haben und lachen kann.

**11** *Musterlösung:*
Es ist schön, wenn man gemeinsame Interessen hat. Eine gute Partnerschaft ist wichtig, weil man nie allein sein muss. Es ist schön, wenn man gemeinsam kocht. Ich finde es wichtig, dass man miteinander über alles reden kann. Besonders wichtig ist, dass man sich nicht über Geld streitet. Eine gute Partnerschaft bedeutet, dass man nicht mit anderen flirtet. Es ist schön, wenn man sich gut kennt. Ich finde es wichtig, dass man sich alles sagen kann. Ich finde es wichtig, dass man den Haushalt gemeinsam macht.

**12** Udo: *denn*; Thomas: *Trotzdem*; Klara: *Deshalb*; Bettina: *aber*

**13** *Musterlösungen:*
**a** *Deshalb* ist er zum Bahnhof gegangen und hat sich eine Fahrkarte gekauft. Vor ihm in der Schlange war ein Mädchen. *Weil* ihm das Mädchen so gut gefallen hat, hat er sie angesprochen und gefragt, ob sie nicht zusammen ins Café gehen könnten. Sie wollte nicht, *denn* sie hatte es eilig. *Trotzdem* haben sie Telefonnummern ausgetauscht und sich für einen Besuch im Café am Wochenende verabredet. *Aber* am Wochenende war Eduard ja in Glasgow. Oje!

**b** Jan und Angelika haben sich letztes Jahr im Urlaub am Strand kennengelernt. *Weil* sie sich auf Anhieb gut verstanden haben, haben sie sich abends für die Disko verabredet. Dort hat Jan Angelika die ganze Zeit ganz verliebt angesehen, *denn* sie hat ihm sehr gefallen. Sie haben schöne gemeinsame Tage verbracht und hatten einen unvergesslichen Urlaub. *Aber weil* sie nach zwei Wochen beide wieder nach Hause fahren mussten, haben sie sich gleich wieder getrennt und sind jeder für sich nach Hause gefahren. Sie waren aber immer noch sehr verliebt. *Deshalb* haben sie sich ein Jahr später wieder getroffen und …

# Answers to the Workbook Exercises

## Wiederholungsstationen

**1** **b** die Übung **c** die Einladung **d** die Bestellung **e** die Wohnung **f** der/die Käufer/-in **g** der/die Fahrer/-in **h** die Empfehlung

**2** der Autobus, der Apfelsaft, der Blumenstrauß, die Sonnenbrille, das Bücherregal, der Busfahrer, die Sonnenblume, der Bücherbus, der Computertisch, das Fahrrad, der Autofahrer, das Spielhaus, der Kleiderschrank, das Mineralwasser, das Wasserrad, der Autoreifen, der Fahrradreifen, der Bücherschrank, der Schreibtisch, das Wohnzimmer …

**3** **b** lesbar **c** unglücklich **d** wolkig **e** regnerisch **f** arbeitslos **g** sonnig **h** dankbar **h** höflich **j** unruhig

**4** **b** einer/eins **c** welche **d** eine **e** keine **f** welche **g** keinen

**5** **b** einen – einen – Einen **c** ein – ein – Ein **d** –

**6** **a** weißer **b** neues – unbequeme – schlechtes – hässliche – niedrigen **c** schönes – großen – kleinen – günstige – billiges – buntes **d** alte – moderne

**7** **a** neuen **b** gutes – kleines **c** Günstige – wunderschöner – ruhiger **d** zentraler – preiswerte – Gute

**8** **b** flachen **c** großes **d** rote **e** interessanter **f** hübschen **g** frisches **h** neue **i** runden **j** kleiner **k** gebrauchte **l** neuen

**9** **a** besser / am besten – besser als – am besten **b** lieber – liebsten **c** am schnellsten – schneller als – schnell wie – billiger **d** wärmer als – kälter

**10** **a** uns **b** dich **c** mich **d** sich

**11** **b** Ihrem Chef **c** eurer Lehrerin **d** seinem Sohn **e** deiner Frau **f** Ihrer Mutter

**12** **b** Könnten Sie bitte der Dame das Zimmer 412 zeigen? – Könnten Sie ihr bitte das Zimmer 412 zeigen? – Könnten Sie es ihr bitte zeigen?
**c** Könnten Sie bitte dem jungen Mann den Hotelparkplatz zeigen? – Könnten Sie ihm bitte den Hotelparkplatz zeigen? – Könnten Sie ihn ihm bitte zeigen?
**d** Könnten Sie bitte der Dame den Koffer tragen? – Könnten Sie ihr bitte den Koffer tragen? – Könnten Sie ihn ihr bitte tragen?
**e** Könnten Sie bitte den Gästen die Rechnungen geben? – Könnten Sie ihnen bitte die Rechnungen geben? – Könnten Sie sie ihnen bitte geben?

**13** *Musterlösung:*
Nachmittags habe ich im Kino angerufen und Kinokarten reserviert. Abends waren wir im Kino und haben uns „Good Bye Lenin" angesehen. Am Dienstag waren wir im Museum. Die Eintrittskarten haben wir am Schalter abgeholt. Danach sind wir ins Café Lisboa gegangen und haben noch einen Stadtbummel gemacht. Am Mittwoch haben wir Lebensmittel für unser Picknick am Freitag eingekauft. Abends sind wir ins Theater gegangen und haben uns das Stück „Frühlingserwachen" angesehen. Am Donnerstag musste ich gleich am Morgen beim Finanzamt anrufen. Um 10.45 Uhr hat unser Schiffsausflug auf dem Sonnensee begonnen. Wir sind um 11.30 Uhr in Brodweil angekommen und waren dann um 16.25 Uhr wieder zurück. Am Freitag haben wir das Auto bei Stefan abgeholt. Wir sind zum Brombacher Weiher gefahren und haben dort ein Picknick gemacht. Am Samstag ist Beate wieder zurück nach Hamburg gefahren. Ich habe sie um 13.30 Uhr zum Bahnhof gebracht. Schade, dass die gemeinsame Zeit schon wieder vorbei ist.

**14** **a** telefoniert – verpasst – begonnen **b** bekommen – erlebt

**15** **a** will **b** hatte – hat **c** war – ist **d** konnte – kann **e** musste – muss

**16** **b** Du solltest einmal Augsburg besuchen. **c** Ihr solltet auch hingehen!

**17** **b** hätte **c** würde **d** wäre **e** hätte **f** würde

**18** **b** Sie werden abgeholt. **c** Jetzt wird endlich die Wohnung aufgeräumt. **d** Eine Kartoffelsuppe wird mit Kartoffeln, Milch und viel Liebe gekocht. **e** Formulare werden bei Frau Müh abgegeben. **f** Hier wird der Müll getrennt.

**19** **b** …schneiden lassen. **c** … machen lassen. **d** … wechseln lassen. **e** … ausstellen lassen.

**20** **b** rein **c** runter **d** raus **e** rauf

**21** **a** Für – dafür **b** worauf – auf einen – darauf **c** Worüber – Über unsere **d** wovon – Von einer **e** Worüber – Über diesen/den

**22** **b** an meinen **c** mit meinen **d** mit meinen **e** um den

**23** **b** anstrengenden **c** seinen **d** einem **e** meine

**24** **b** auf dem – auf den **c** an die **d** zwischen das – den **e** auf dem

**25** **a** am Bodensee, in Italien, auf der Insel Mallorca, in der Türkei, bei meinen Eltern auf dem Land, im Norden, zu Hause **b** ins Kino, zu meinem Freund, ins Restaurant, nach Hause **c** vom Arzt, aus dem / vom Büro, vom Strand, von ihrer Schwester, aus dem Restaurant, aus dem Gebirge, aus Österreich

**26** **a** über – an **b** an … vorbei – gegenüber **c** durch – um … herum

**27** **b** Von … an **c** ohne **d** über **e** Von … an

**28** **b** Deshalb **c** denn **d** Weil **e** denn **f** deshalb

**29** **b** weil **c** wenn/weil **d** wenn **e** weil **f** Trotzdem

**30** **b** wann **c** wo **d** wie lange **e** was **f** wie viele

**31** **b** ob **c** ob **d** dass **e** dass **f** ob

# Answers to the Workbook Exercises

## Start Deutsch 2 – Die Prüfung

### Hören

| 1 | 2 | 3 | 4 | 5 | 6 | 7 | 8 | 9 | 10 | 11 | 12 | 13 | 14 | 15 |
|---|---|---|---|---|---|---|---|---|----|----|----|----|----|----|
| Mozart-straße | 98 Euro | 9602333 | Café | Mai | c | b | c | b | b | f | c | e | b | h |

### Lesen 1

| 1 | 2 | 3 | 4 | 5 |
|---|---|---|---|---|
| b | c | a | a | c |

### Lesen 2

| 6 | 7 | 8 | 9 | 10 |
|---|---|---|---|----|
| Falsch | Falsch | Richtig | Falsch | Richtig |

### Lesen 3

| 11 | 12 | 13 | 14 | 15 |
|----|----|----|----|----|
| f | g | b | — | c |

### Schreiben 1

| 1 | 2 | 3 | 4 | 5 |
|---|---|---|---|---|
| NL-1017 Amsterdam | 24.12.1984 | männlich | 1. Juni | Hessen |

### Schreiben 2

*Musterlösung:*

Lieber Marco,

wie schön, dass du mich besuchen kommst. Ich freue mich auch schon sehr auf unser Wiedersehen. Wir können bei meinen Eltern wohnen, es gibt genug Platz.

Ich schlage vor, dass wir uns erst einmal meine Heimatstadt ein wenig ansehen. Wir könnten auch ein paar Tage aufs Land fahren und im Sommerhaus von meinen Großeltern wohnen. Das Wetter ist bestimmt gut, denn es ist ja Sommer. Aber auch wenn es regnet, macht das nichts, wenn du die richtige Kleidung mitbringst. Am besten packst du eine Regenjacke und feste Schuhe ein, dann können wir auch bei schlechtem Wetter rausgehen.

Ich wünsche dir eine gute Reise und freue mich sehr auf dich.

Viele Grüße

dein(e) ...